THE SECRET OF NUMBERS REVEALED

The Magic Power of Numbers

Restored, Revised, and Edited by

CATHERINE YRONWODE

From the Original Writings of

DR. ROY PAGE WALTON
LEWIS DE CLAREMONT
GODFREY SPENCER &
FRANK HOUSEHOLDER

cat yronwode

Lucky Mojo Library of Occult Classics
Lucky Mojo Curio Company
Forestville, California
2019

The Secret of Numbers Revealed:
The Magic Power of Numbers
by Catherine Yronwode, Dr. Roy Page Walton,
Lewis de Claremont, Godfrey Spencer, and Frank Householder

Earlier editions comprising about half of this book were published under the titles
Names, Dates, and Numbers: What They Mean To You by Dr. Roy Page Walton in 1914,
How To Get Your Winning Number by Lewis de Claremont in 1938,
and *The Secret of Numbers Revealed* by Godfrey Spencer in 1939.

Text:
Catherine Yronwode, Dr. Roy Page Walton,
Lewis de Claremont, Godfrey Spencer, and Frank Householder

Editor:
catherine yronwode

Cover Art:
Greywolf Townsend
Front: Charles C. Dawson (Art and Lettering), Charles M. Quinlan (Additional Lettering),
Back: Unknown Letterer for George Sully & Co., nagasiva yronwode

Typesetting:
catherine yronwode

Interior Illustrations:
Charles M. Quinlan for Empire Publishing, Unknown Artist and Letterer for Edward J. Clode,
Unknown Artist and Letterer for George Sully & Co., nagasiva yronwode

Production:
nagasiva yronwode

First Edition 2019

Published by
The Lucky Mojo Curio Company
6632 Covey Road
Forestville, California 95436
LuckyMojo.com

ISBN: 978-0-9997809-3-0

Printed in Canada.

CONTENTS

DEDICATION

This book is dedicated to Mrs. Hare, who taught me Numerology in the Summer of 1955, and to Dr. Roy Page Walton, an honest Numerologist whose work was plagiarized by the man who called himself Lewis de Claremont, Louis de Clairemont, Godfrey Spencer, and Mr. Young.

ACKNOWLEDGEMENTS

What an interesting journey the compilation, restoration, and expansion of this old book has been! As always, i've had much help and inspiration:

Thank you, Mrs. Hare, for taking the time to teach an eight year old girl the science of Numerology from an early edition of this book. Everything you said was right and true, and all has come to pass as you foretold.

Thank you, Peter Yronwode, for being a Kabbalist after my own heart and spending such happy, hopeful days in the pursuit of the perfect couple-name. Our paths may have diverged, but our chosen name lives on!

Thank you, nagasiva yronwode, for joining the ragtime band; for art scans and restoration; for playing the Valentine's Day Lo Shu Square Permutations Game with me; for proofreading, production, and printer-wrangling; and, of course, for the morning coffee and apple slices.

In addition to Dr. Roy Page Walton, whose *Names, Dates, and Numbers* forms the core of this book, i wish to thank Mrs. L. Dow Balliett, Malcolm Madison, Walter B. Gibson, Karen Adams, Clifford W. Cheasley, Robert A. Nelson, Richie Piazza, Juno Jordan, Frank Householder, Lars Berglund, Ron Martin Shank, Larry Baukin, Lillian Too, Richard Webster, and Dennis Perez, who have cast light on my sometimes shadowed numerical path.

Thanks to Greywolf Townsend for the speedy and clean art restoration for our new cover and interior artwork. You are a wizard, sir.

Thanks to my faithful proofreaders Katrink Karpetz, Fred Burke, and Holly Windsong Greenwood. I am grateful to rely on your good eyes.

And, finally, thanks to the team at the Lucky Mojo Curio Co. who kept our business on track while i was shut up in my little room spinning straw into gold: Leslie Lowell, Eileen Edler, Heidi Simpson, Nikki Wilson, Yosé Witmus, Margee Stephenson, Nicole Carevich, Jenne Nelson, Ernie Medeiros, Althea Anderson, Holly Windsong Greenwood, Rowena Sparks, Bailey Margarit-Lowell, and Angela Marie Horner.

PREFACE TO THE PRESENT EDITION

The Secret of Numbers Revealed, originally published in 1938 in the form of a 48-page pamphlet called *How To Get Your Winning Number*, has always held a fond place in my heart. I first encountered it in 1955, when i was eight years old. It was one of dozens of esoteric books and pamphlets on fortune telling and psychic reading neatly arrayed on the bottom shelf of the glass-fronted cabinet of Mrs. Hare, a neighbour who watched me after school while my mother was at work.

Mrs. Hare was a psychic. She read cards, taught me the basics of Palmistry, Tea Leaf Reading, and Astrology, and she used Numerology, as expounded by Godfrey Spencer and Dr. Korda RaMayne, to tell my character and predict my future according to my name and birth date. She told me i would travel widely in search of occult knowledge, that i had a gift for psychic work, and that i would become a writer.

I was still in grade school and took her prophesies with a grain of salt. However, her character analysis was so accurate, and Numerology seemed so easy to perform, that i began to use it at once. With the help of *The Secret of Numbers Revealed*, i was able to create work-outs on the names of my school friends as an intriguing amusement. Numerology won me over, and it has held a strong place in my heart ever since.

It was only a few years later that i realized that all of Mrs. Hare's prophesies about my life, which were quite specific, were slowly coming true, just as she had foretold. I had begun to travel in search of folklore.

At that time, every hoodoo drugstore, herbal pharmacy, incense store, and candle shop i entered carried a sideline of booklets on folk magic and folkloric forms of divination. *The Secret of Numbers Revealed,* along with *The Master Book of Candle Burning, The Magical Formula for Successful Prayer, 25 Lessons in Hypnotism, Aunt Sally's Policy Players Dream Book, The Ten Lost Books of the Prophets, Pow-Wows or The Long-Lost Friend, Black and White Magic of Marie Laveau, The Sixth and Seventh Books of Moses, Secrets of the Psalms, Seven Keys to Power, Six Lessons in Crystal Gazing, The Long-Lost 8th, 9th, and 10th Books of Moses, The Guiding Light to Power and Success, Egyptian Secrets of Albertus Magnus, Prof. Hitt's' Rundowns and Workouts, How I Discovered My Mediumship,* and *Legends of Incense, Herb, and Oil Magic* served to introduce me to the written world of popular American occultism.

These occult booklets were available nationwide, in every conjure shop i entered. The shops catered to an African-American customer base, and the central religion touched upon in these esoteric texts was Christianity, with an emphasis on the Old Testament (which i, as a Jew, recognized as Judaism), augmented by Christian Spiritualism and New Thought.

I read them all, and many others like them, and i understood them to be a transformative upwelling within a uniquely Black form of folk magic. When i asked older African-American practitioners to teach me how to work, i recognized that some of the spells and prayers they gave me were similar to material in the books, either because the books drew upon and documented an even older generation of hoodoo practice, or because the books were influencing the course of hoodoo, in the same way that new songs influence the course of popular music. By the time i came along, in the 1960s, these books, mostly published between 1820 and 1948, were both casting light upon and drawing light from the previous generations of hoodoo rootworkers among whom i travelled and from whom i learned.

I first bought my own copy of *The Secret of Numbers Revealed* by Godfrey Spencer in 1961, in Oakland, California. A few years later, i was in Chicago and saw a copy there. Then on to New York, Saint Louis, Los Angeles, Philadelphia, Atlanta, San Antonio, Houston, and Detroit. The book, with its cheerful yellow cover (later a sad beige), was everywhere.

At some point in my travels, however, i found a beat-up copy of a different pamphlet on Numerology in a used book store. This was *How To Get Your Winning Number* by Lewis de Claremont, a name i recognized as the author of *Seven Keys to Power* and *Legends of Incense, Herb, and Oil Magic* — as well as the proprietor of a defunct but well-remembered New-York-based spiritual supply house of the 1930s called the Oracle Products Craftsmen (OPC). As "Mr. Young," this same man was also the originator of Young's Chinese Wash, a liquid cleaner so highly valued that after the demise of the OPC, every hoodoo manufactory from the Clover Horn in Baltimore to Papa Jim's in San Antonio made their own version of it.

Imagine my shock when i opened up the red and black cover of *How To Get Your Winning Number* by Lewis de Claremont and recognized the exact same text that i knew so well from *The Secret of Numbers Revealed* by Godfrey Spencer. I just kept shaking my head. If this was plagiarism, surely Godfrey Spencer — whoever he was — would have had Lewis de Claremont up on charges and in jail forthwith — or vice versa!

The original 1938 cover of *How To Get Your Winning Number* by Lewis de Claremont, signed by the comic book artist Charles M. Quinlan.

My mother was a librarian and my folks also ran an antiquarian bookstore, so my home training as a bibliographic researcher kicked in. I started collecting variant editions of both books, comparing them for telltale signs of broken type, text corrections, and repagination — and what i found was bizarre, to say the least.

Both of these pamphlets were stone-cold, word-for-word plagiarisms of a much earlier book — a slender hard-cover volume titled *Names, Dates, and Numbers: What They Mean To You* by Dr. Roy Page Walton, published by Edward J. Clode in New York City in 1914!

The earliest pirated edition of Walton's book was published in 1938 by Joseph Spitalnick's Empire Publishing as *How To Get Your Winning Number.* The author named on the cover, and on page 48, was Lewis de Claremont. The cover art was signed by Charles M. Quinlan, a New York City comic book artist who also drew the cover and interior illustrations for de Claremont's *Legends of Incense, Herb, and Oil Magic,* and produced all of the OPC catalogue art and product labels from 1936 through 1939.

Interestingly, in addition to the text of *Names, Dates, and Numbers* in its uncredited entirety, *How To Get Your Winning Number* also contained an original chapter on lucky numbers for illegal Policy or Numbers games.

Two more editions of *How To Get Your Winning Number* followed from Empire Publishing, in 1938 and 1939. Each was only 32 pages long, but they were not re-typeset. Rather, entire pages were simply omitted — often breaking off in the middle of a sentence! — and the defects were crudely covered by renumbering the pages in sequence, as if nothing had been cut. Not only that, each edition was missing *different* pages, and the 1939 cover was not printed in red and black, but from a muddy black and white photo of the 1938 cover, as if the line art or plates had been lost. The page signed "Lewis de Claremont" was on page 30 in both of these truncated booklets. My sense is that Joseph Spitalnick (who also was known as Joe Kay) stapled loose overage signatures to make quickie pseudo-books for sale.

In 1938 and 1939, *The Secret of Numbers Revealed* by Godfrey Spencer was released by Empire and also by Pyramid Publishing. Both editions were 48 pages long, with covers printed on heavy leatherette (tan for Empire and bright yellow for Pyramid). Along with the new title came a new cover by Charles C. Dawson, a highly accomplished designer and painter who produced label and catalogue art for Morton G. Neumann's Famous Products, King Novelty Company, and Valmor Beauty Supplies in Chicago.

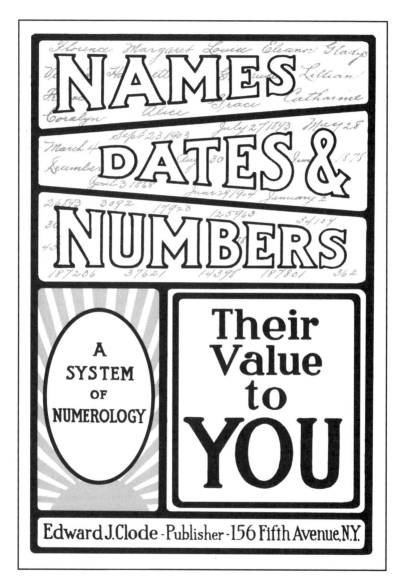

The original 1914 dust wrapper to *Names, Dates, and Numbers: What They Mean To You* by Dr. Roy Page Walton. Artist Unknown.

Why the name change? I think Neumann bought entire press runs of the book under two conditions — first, that his own designer create a new cover, and second, that the implied endorsement of illegal gambling, as exemplified in the title *How To Get Your Winning Number,* be quieted. De Claremont's name was removed from page 48, and a few typesetting errors were corrected, but the content was otherwise the same.

Also dated 1939 were two editions from Dorene Publishing, N.Y., of *The Secret of Numbers Revealed* by Godfrey Spencer. Issued with plain index stock wraps (rust brown on one, dull beige on the other), and 48 pages long, they still contained Lewis de Claremont's name on page 48.

In 1969, Dorene, now located in Dallas, Texas, published a revised edition. The only difference from earlier Dorene versions was that the pagination was in Helvetica type for the first time, and the booklet was now 56 pages long — the original 48 pages plus 8 pages of advertisements.

Since Dorene stopped printing the book in the early 2000s, a few abortive attempts have been made to get one version or another back into a print-on-demand release, but no one has wanted to restore the broken type, correct the typos, or fix the computational errors which have remained in place since 1938. I guess i am just the fool enough to do it, even knowing that demand will be limited and ignorant folks will say, "It's all available for free on the internet." But the truth is — it isn't.

What you hold in your hands now is a 96-page edition of Dr. Roy Page Walton's 1914 book, *Names, Dates, and Numbers: What They Mean To You.* It is exactly twice the length of *How To Get Your Winning Number* or, as i first knew it, *The Secret of Numbers Revealed.* I had originally planned to simply add my own 48 page book to it, but as i got deeper into the project, i realized that after more than 60 years as a Numerologist, i had a lot to say in support of, and in commentary to, Dr. Roy Page Walton.

All of this came together when i realized that Walton's chapter on pseudonyms was slyly autobiographical. At that point my mission changed. What was conceived as a reprint project become a dialogue with the dead, a duet after the manner of Natalie Cole singing harmony with her long departed father, Nat "King" Cole. At first i fancied using contrasting type fonts to keep our individual voices distinct. But then i remembered that i am a number 11 with an ungodly number of hidden 5s, and my Lo Shu Square features the Line of Intellect and the Line of Self-Assurance, so i just said, "Ah, well. This is a teaching book, and i am a teacher, so here it is."

A MAP OF SORTS

This book covers five topics: **Numerology** or numerical character analysis, **Arithmancy** or fortune telling by numbers, **Number Magic** or manipulating the name to increase good fortune, **Lucky Numbers** or winning digits for betting, and **Spiritual Numberology** or Gematria.

Chapters 1 - 7, 12 - 13, and 15 - 16 are the work of Dr. Roy Page Walton, with a great many additions by me. Chapters 8 - 11, 14, and 17 - 18 are of my own devising. Chapter 19 is by "Lewis de Claremont," with additions by me. Chapter 20 is mine. Chapter 21 is by me, with zodiacal notes by Walter B. Gibson, plus extracts from *The Mystic Fortune Teller* by the Wehman Bros. Chapter 22 is mine, with additional material supplied by the Biblical numerologist Frank Householder.

— CATHERINE YRONWODE

DR. ROY PAGE WALTON'S INTRODUCTION

The tremendous interest taken of late in names and numbers may be described as phenomenal.

This widely spreading interest may be ascribed to the fact that the present civilization is very desirous of learning of self, and reaches out eagerly for any subject that can help in human deduction, and that simplicity of this method of self-analysis naturally attracts to itself an ever increasing and enthusiastic following.

While it is true the large majority of people are really seeking for a solution regarding life, with a desire to obey that God-given command: "Man, Know Thyself," there also exists a certain class of individuals who use this and other means of entertainment.

I wish this volume to be accepted as representing one channel of human analysis; also as a source of entertainment as well as instruction, for what can be more interesting and fascinating than an unbiased analysis of self?

The study of Names and Numbers opens up a new and large field in the hidden world of self-analysis, gives to us many facts pertaining to our individuality, and also suplies a reason for apparent success or failure that heretofore was impossible to be obtained.

— THE AUTHOR

CHAPTER ONE
THE LAW OF NUMBERS

Nothing in this Universe of sorrows and joys is more intensely interesting or fascinating than that collection of atoms attuned to move at human vibration, the vibration-being commonly called "Self."

This self is a persevering and consistent seeker, a seeker many times for recognition, for flattery, and for praise, but, in reality, a seeker for real knowledge that it may better probe and learn of that mysterious entity, termed "Self," and the true position of its self amongst the unexplainable laws and powers of nature, which are commonly called "Life's Riddles."

In answer to humanity's call for an explanation of the laws everywhere about, and for an explanation of the relation of the self to nature, many great minds have responded with the subjects of Astrology, Palmistry, and Psychometry — and humanity has decided, after much investigation, that all these subjects serve a purpose and, in their way, are beneficial and useful, because they reveal much that is instructive and helpful.

But, for simplicity and usefulness, the subject of Numerology is destined to fill a bigger want as it covers a larger field in the education of man than any other system of character analysis and divination.

Because the study of numbers is divided into these two great principles — investigations into human character and the prediction and possession of good luck — our study here will follow along those lines.

The first and greatest lesson to be mastered consists of gaining insight into what the numbers mean and what influence they possess. After this, we will use a series of simple numerological techniques to:

- **Reduce multiple-digit numbers** to a common digit for analysis.
- **Apply numbers to names and dates,** and then reduce them.
- **Learn how to assess harmonious and discordant numbers,** or those that are in mutual alliance or antagonistic to one another.
- **Find lucky winning numbers** in names, dates, dreams, and omens.
- **Change or choose names and their spellings** to beneficially affect success in career, marriage, and set children on a good path in life.
- **Investigate spiritual numbers** that have been hidden in plain sight.

We will begin with a study of the character of each of the numbers.

CHAPTER TWO
THE CHARACTER OF THE NUMBERS

THE CHARACTER AND INFLUENCE OF NUMBER 1

One is a strong, forceful, active, creative, and masculine number. It represents unity, individuality, originality, self-awareness, and leadership. As the first number, it represents all beginnings. Courageous, bold, and brave, it cannot be said to "hide its light under a bushel."

The typical One individual analyzes everything by his standard of life and refuses to accept anything his five senses cannot include or understand. One is a number of ego, ruling, directing, inventing, centralizing, and planning. It radiates the do-and-dare spirit, but may become officious and dominating, refusing to recognize or consider any difficulties, obstacles or barriers, and it rides right over anything or any person in its way. To the negative, it can be selfish, petulant, self-centered, and fail to recognize anything beyond its own, often very limited, vision.

One was the powerful foundation-stone of creation and retains much of its original austerity and rulership. It is symbolized by the Sun.

THE CHARACTER AND INFLUENCE OF NUMBER 2

Number Two is distinctly feminine, receptive, and unselfish. It radiates an intuitive, nourishing, and maternal quality. It seeks justice.

Although it embodies duality, it is a kind, sympathetic, diplomatic, and peace-loving number, showing concern for others, and flexibility in negotiations. While Two is far from being a real power in its influence, it is always protective to those in its care. Its strength is more subjective than objective. Its influence is refined, gentle, and helpful. Number Two is said to be the ideal number for mothers, doctors, dentists, nurses, arbitrators, and diplomats. It excels at giving assistance to those in need.

It is a vibration of good temperament, a number more of the heart than the mind. Its chief weaknesses are placid passivity and procrastination.

Charm, endearment, affection, and attachment are words that describe the Number Two influence, and it bestows composure, calm, and companionship in all friendly associations. It is symbolized by the Moon.

THE CHARACTER AND INFLUENCE OF NUMBER 3

Three is a number of expression, declamation, and enunciation. It influences oratory, acting, singing, writing, dancing, and painting.

Its principal characteristics are activity, mirth, good cheer, merriment, artistry, and jollity. Sincere gladness, pleasure, ecstasy, and inspiration are among its predominating expressions. Number Three is said to be the joy-giving number. It is versatile, popular, exuberant, and generally free from worry. Its enthusiasm is contagious, and Three people attract many friends by means of their wit and verbal facility.

The negative qualities of Three consist of a fascination with action and novelty that may lead to a lack of focus, both in career and in the building of long-term relationships. Worse, when hard times come, as some day they will, the ever-optimistic Three may be unable to overcome the challenges that other numbers have grown used to in their less brilliant lives. When the Three loses its sunny disposition and becomes indifferent, it will do well to call upon compassionate and supportive friends and family to help ease the way from darkness back into the light. Its planet is Mars.

THE CHARACTER AND INFLUENCE OF NUMBER 4

Four bestows a discerning and tenacious influence on its bearer. It is a physical number, solid, logical, strong in it foundations, and much given to analysis and discussion. It is not known for its wit, and some may find its steadiness boring, but Four does possess a dry sense of humour.

It is a good vibration in many ways on which to undertake a venture, as it is strong, persistent, steadfast, and hard to turn from its course. The old saying, "On four squares the city stands," holds much truth.

Four is a number of patient accumulation, gleaning, collection, and material concentration, and it loves to possess for possession's sake. In its undeveloped state, Four is a pugnacious, unrefined, concrete, practical, and physically enduring number that curbs and restrains all things that are not natural or scientific. However, there is no harder or more dedicated worker than a Four, and it is a great defender of home and country.

The Four will not procrastinate, it will toil ceaselessly, and it can be trusted with management responsibilities. The detailed memorization capacities of the Four may be remarkably persistent. Its planet is Mercury.

THE CHARACTER AND INFLUENCE OF NUMBER 5

The number Five represents the five senses, tending toward excitement, nervousness, and tempestuousness. It is double-sided and may be compared to a man sitting upon a fence, leaning first one way and then another, never certain in which direction his best interests lie. It predicts more than one marriage and denotes a love of travel and new scenes.

Five is called the number of hypnotists, astrologers, and magicians. Being two-sided, it is both constructive and destructive, optimistic and pessimistic, cheerful and melancholy, spiritual and material. It is a number of entertainment, light talk, fashion, dexterity, and variety, lacking stability. It investigates the unseen or mystical for the sake of knowledge, not to increase productivity. It is changeable, adaptable, intelligent, and quick.

It brings a fascination with the bizarre which is said to be unlucky, but this may be due to the old idea that a thing which could not be explained must be unlucky, just as in olden times a witch was condemned when she performed acts beyond the understanding of her neighbours and her work was wrongly seen as ungodly. It is symbolized by Jupiter.

THE CHARACTER AND INFLUENCE OF NUMBER 6

The number Six is peace-loving, optimistic, joy-giving, kind, and considerate. It is more universal than personal in scope, and it influences art, philanthropy, intuition, and inspiration. It promotes the so-called sixth sense, or metaphysical perceptivity, and is associated with the gifts of clairvoyance and healing. Its influence in financial matters is doubtful, but its influence in health and religion is strong and dependable. It holds to high ideals, and, although peaceful, it will fight for what is right.

Six bestows confidence, trust, and reliance in others, proclaiming, "United we stand, divided we fall." Weak when unattended, but powerful when in combination, it also tells us that, "Strength united is stronger."

Its most negative consequences are a vain and sanctimonious piety which may develop as so many people ask the Six to help, an over-expenditure of compassion as it sincerely does seek to help and comfort all who approach it, and a tendency to dwell in realms of fantasy.

It is a number of marriage, as well as one of beauty, comprehension, conservatism, solace, and comfort. It is symbolized by Venus.

THE CHARACTER AND INFLUENCE OF NUMBER 7

Number Seven is a mysterious, magical, obscure, unaccountable number, and it is probably considered such because its influence is not thoroughly understood. As an indivisible number, it works best when solitary. It is a number of surface affability, self-satisfaction, and outward poise that does not actively seek out business partnerships or friendships, and even when married, it preserves itself as a partial mystery.

The root or origin of the Seven is a vibration "in the world, but not of the world." It is not a number to seek renown or glory, or any form of self-expression. Throughout time the Seven influence has been dark, obscure, secret and hidden, always in its glow, dim and enigmatical.

Retirement, seclusion, solitude, privacy, self-discipline, repose, and retreat are common words used in describing this Seven influence.

It is an important number, leading back, as it does, to the soul, to essential truths, and to the quiet, poised, and unexpressed self of man. It demonstrates that state of conscience called self-sufficiency. It is the number of the stoic, the religionist, and the mystic. Its planet is Saturn.

THE CHARACTER AND INFLUENCE OF NUMBER 8

Eight is a scientific, mental number of business, material achievement, self-assertiveness, and success. It radiates inclusiveness, accomplishment, attainment, and acquirement, and spreads an aura of discernment, analysis, and technicality. Its mission is acquisition, achievement, and execution, and as a high, free number, it has universal sympathy and understanding.

In choosing a name to appear under as a singer, musician, or artist, do not accept the number Eight as a good choice, but if Eight is applied as a name for use in business or as a lawyer, one may expect help from its material and mental power, for it gives rather a "self-positive" atmosphere.

It is a number of domination and transformation; it tends towards organization and intellectuality, and it should create a good influence for the investor, the manager, the scientist, the technician, and those who have charge over the work of others. Because it seeks success in the materialistic realm, the Eight must learn not to plunge into wild speculations. It should utilize management skills to experience its desired fulfillment.

The mighty, powerful, potent vibration of business, its planet is Uranus.

THE CHARACTER AND INFLUENCE OF NUMBER 9

Nine is known as the number of regeneration and honest truth, representing the highest essence of universal and personal love. It is not ambitious or materialistic, yet it extends a high, broad, universal influence.

As One is the beginning and Nine the ending of numbers, so are they as far apart in their influences; for One represents individuality and Nine represents universality, geniality, and standing for uprightness, integrity, and virtue: it is a permanent, enduring, and steadfast number.

The Nine is well equipped to face the existing circumstances of daily living. It has an influence for expression, especially in art, and is a helpful influence for the actor, singer, speaker, or judge; in fact along any line of expression, being in this respect similar to the Three.

The developed Nine loves knowledge and is inclusive, never petty, small, or personal. Even if undeveloped and given to vague dreaminess, the Nine has much universal love, which means love for the low as well as for the high, which sees God in all things and all conditions. Its influence on others is generally perceived as beneficial. It is symbolized by Neptune.

THE CHARACTER OF THE MASTER NUMBERS 11, 22, 33

The Master Numbers are double-digit numbers in which both digits are identical. Some numerologists do not work with Master Numbers at all, but most acknowledge that there are three of them — 11, 22, and 33. A few writers add 44, 55, 66, 77, 88, and 99 to the set, but most do not do so.

11 is the so-called "Old Soul" number. It conveys intelligence, wisdom, original thinking, gifted intuition, sacred knowledge, spiritual sensitivity, and supernatural abilities, as well as empathy held within a calm, steady mind. Number 11 is connected with psychic readers and diviners.

22 is the so-called "Master Builder" number. It is associated with the application of practical ideas and visionary insights to the achievement of broad humanitarian goals. As a practical number, 22 conveys the ability to align diverse people in service to great undertakings.

33 is the so-called "Great Teacher" number. It harnesses emotion and creativity to simplify cosmic principles for ease of understanding as it guides others through complex and difficult projects. Number 33 is excitable and joyous, and derives great pleasure from teaching.

CHAPTER THREE
REDUCTION AND APPLICATION:
THE BASIC TECHNIQUES OF NUMEROLOGY

REDUCING COMPOUND NUMBERS TO SINGLE DIGITS

There are only nine numbers or numerals, any total above these single-digit numbers being simply a combination or union of numbers.

For example, the number 18 is a combination of 1 and 8, and the number 57 is a combination of 5 and 7. These are compound numbers. They are not vibrational or numbers in the sense that the digits 1 and 9 inclusive are, but rather a union of several numbers.

In applying numbers to names or dates, compound numbers are brought down or reduced to a single unit. To illustrate: take the number 67. Reducing it, we have 6 plus 7 = 13; but now, as 13 is still a union of 1 and 3 and a compound number, we again add and find that 1 plus 3 = 4; hence, the digit value of 67 reduces to 4 (6 plus 7 =13, then 1 plus 3 = 4).

Another example: 552 is to be reduced to a single digit as it is composed of three numbers. To find its working value we add 5 plus 5 plus 2 = 12; and as 12 is still a union of numbers we add again 1 plus 2 = 3. Hence the reduction of 552 is 3 (5 plus 5 plus 2 = 12; 1 plus 2 = 3).

THE IRREDUCIBLE MASTER NUMBERS

It is a commonplace that all number combinations over 9 in value are to be reduced to a single digit, and that these single digits are from 1 to 9 inclusive. However, there is an exception to this supposed rule, which may or may not be invoked by any given numerologist, according to belief, custom, and the use to which the number reduction is to be applied.

According to this exception, there are several double-digit numbers, the so-called Master Numbers, which should not, or need not, be reduced.

The irreducible Master Numbers cited by experienced numerologists are 11, 22, and 33. In addition, a few practitioners do not reduce 44, 55, 66, 77, 88, or 99 on the grounds that these too are Master Numbers.

If Master Numbers are the sums of the first, middle, or last name, they are reduced when enumerating the full name, but they should be noted.

THE 123-ABC KEY: APPLYING NUMBERS TO LETTERS

Numerologists apply numbers to words, especially to names or nouns. This application may be done for personal spiritual purposes such as numerical character reading, discovering hidden similarities and differences between words or people, and for the predictive value of numbers in relationship to other numbers, whether those be dates or numerals used in game-play.

When we convert a word to a number, we begin by transferring a number to every letter. There are several ways to make this transference, depending on the alphabet one starts with, or the complexity of the number system one is utilizing.

For convenience sake, we will begin with the simplest and best-known version in the English language, the "123-ABC" or Master Key method. Fully 90% or more of the working numerologists in the United States of America use this method, and derive pleasure and profit thereby.

To make the transference from letters to numbers, the alphabet is divided as follows — and for your help in memorization, a well-known mnemonic set of phrases is appended, should you care to use it:

1 -	A	J	S	*("One-A, Just So")*
2 -	B	K	T	*("Two Buckets")*
3 -	C	L	U	*("Three Clues")*
4 -	D	M	V	*("For the DMV" [Department of Motor Vehicles])*
5 -	E	N	W	*("South, East, North, West" [5 resembles an S])*
6 -	F	O	X	*("666, the Number of the Beast — a Fox")*
7 -	G	P	Y	*("Seven Gypsies")*
8 -	H	Q	Z	*("Eight Headquarters")*
9 -	I	R		*("Niner")*

The 26 alphabetic letters of the English language are not placed haphazardly opposite their corresponding numbers, but rather they follow in a set rotation of valuation, just as do numbers.

For instance, Y is a 7 because it is the 25th letter in the alphabet and the value of 25 is 7, as 2 plus 5 = 7.

Likewise, L is a 3 because it is the 12th letter in the alphabet and the single digit of 12 is 3, as 1 plus 2 = 3.

APPLYING NUMBERS TO NAMES

If, in applying numbers to names, you wish to find the single unit value of a whole name, you may place under each letter its number value, and reduce them thus, which is called a draw-down or work-out:

J	O	H	N		A	P	P	E	L	L
1	6	8	5		1	7	7	5	3	3

20   26

2   **8**

2 plus 8 = 10, and as 1 plus 0 = 1, so **1** is the number of John Appell.

A name can be "numberized" in whole, as above, or by its parts, as below. The separation or parsing of a name into its parts may be useful if one contemplates a name change.

J is 1
O is 6
H is 8
N is 5

20 is the total, and 2 plus 0 = 2, so the single digit of John is **2.**

A Vibrates to 1
P Vibrates to 7
P Vibrates to 7
E Vibrates to 5
L Vibrates to 3
L Vibrates to 3

26 is the total, and 2 plus 6 = 8, hence Appell vibrates to **8.**

To check our work, we can add 2, which is John's valuation, to 8 which is Appell's valuation, and we have 2 plus 8 = 10, and 10 is 1 because 1 plus 0 = 1, so the name John Appell vibrates to the number **1,** whether drawn down by its whole or parsed by its parts.

APPLYING NUMBERS TO DATES

Applying numbers to dates may seem strange, because dates are already composed of numbers, but we will, in accordance with the principles of Numerology, reduce those dates to a single digit. This is a typical example:

December 19, 1884
 December is the 12th month: 1 plus 2 = **3.**
 The 19th day: 1 plus 9 = 10, then 1 plus 0 = **1.**
 The year 1884: 1 plus 8 plus 8 plus 4 = 21, and 2 plus 1 = **3.**
 3 plus 1 plus 3 = **7** — and that is the number of this date.
Simplified, the date is **12-19-1884**, and the resultant sum is the same:
12 plus 19 plus 1884 = 1915; 1 plus 9 plus 1 plus 5 = 16; 1 plus 6 = **7.**

Numbers and reduction can be applied to a wide variety of dates:

• **The Birth Date:** This date is used in character analysis and in some systems of prediction for lucky numbers, as well as when selecting days for undertakings that harmonize with one's natural inclination.
• **The Wedding Date:** Planning a wedding calls for the selection of an auspicious date, and if you know the names and birth dates of both bride and groom, a suitable date can be determined with a few calculations.
• **The Date to Open a Business:** Like the wedding date, this is calculated from the birth date and name numbers of the principles. A fortuitous first day for a business helps set the tone for the entire enterprise.
• **Lucky Days:** These are days selected for gambling play, embarking on vacations, and having advantage in every way. Not all lucky day calculations involve the birth date, but many do take it into account.

A REVIEW OF THE BASIC TECHNIQUES

1. We reduce multiple-digit numbers by adding them to get a single digit.
2. The Master Numbers 11, 22, and 33 need not or should not be reduced.
3. We apply numbers to letters, names, and words and then reduce them.
4. We express dates as numbers and reduce them as we do with words.

We are now ready to begin the actual practice of Numerology.

CHAPTER FOUR
THE KEY AND THE KEYWORDS

THE VITAL INFORMATION YOU WILL NEED

Here, on one page, is the 123-ABC Key for working out names, the memory system, the monthly date-codes, and the keywords for the character of the numbers. Carry a copy in your wallet as you learn.

```
1 2 3 4 5 6 7 8 9
A B C D E F G H I
J K L M N O P Q R
S T U V W X Y Z
```

1 - A	J	S	("One-A, Just So")	1 - Jan Oct
2 - B	K	T	("Two Buckets")	2 - Feb Nov
3 - C	L	U	("Three Clues")	3 - Mar Dec
4 - D	M	V	("For the DMV")	4 - Apr
5 - E	N	W	("South, East, North, West")	5 - May
6 - F	O	X	("666, the Number of the Fox")	6 - Jun
7 - G	P	Y	("Seven Gypsies")	7 - Jul
8 - H	Q	Z	("Eight Headquarters")	8 - Aug
9 - I	R		("Niner")	9 - Sep

1 Adventurous, bold, brave, a leader, an innovator.
2 Receptive, gentle, diplomatic, peaceable, calm.
3 Expressive, enthusiastic, joyous, inspirational.
4 Practical, scientific, accumulative, hard-working.
5 Changeable, adaptable, in motion, quick, dextrous.
6 Humanitarian, compassionate, helpful, supportive.
7 Introspective, quiet, meditative, reclusive, poised.
8 Organized, acquisitive, financially successful.
9 Universal, artistic, upright, virtuous, enduring.

11 Intelligent, wise, a gifted and intuitive psychic.
22 Visionary, a planner of great cooperative tasks.
33 A teacher of cosmic principles, a creative guide.

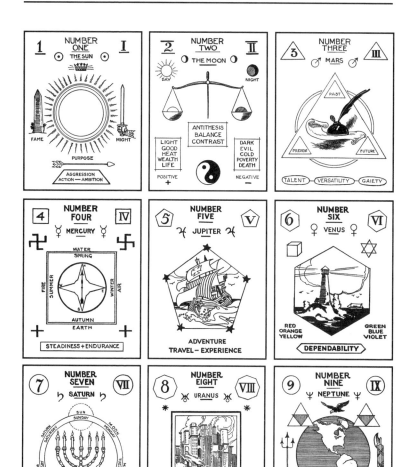

Mnemonic illustrations for the numbers 1 through 9, from *The Science of Numerology* by Walter B. Gibson, 1927. Artist Unknown. Walter Brown Gibson (1897-1985) was a stage magician and author. Under the pseudonym "Maxwell Grant" he penned more than 300 novel-length stories of the pulp fiction detective *The Shadow*. He also wrote comic books, radio dramas, and works on metaphysics and the occult.

CHAPTER FIVE
THE MEANING OF THE NAME NUMBERS

CHARACTER ANALYSIS OF A SINGLE NICKNAME

The most common use of Numerology is in the production of a character analysis. By that term is meant an understanding of the otherwise undisclosed inner nature of a person, as evidenced in the name.

However, while the inner character of a name is not a divination or telling of the future, it can be used to gain insight into another person's life.

First, people tend to follow habitual patterns, so a character analysis may have predictive value. For example, we can say with some degree of assurance that a man who takes inordinate risks while driving may some day suffer an accident. We cannot predict when it will happen, but we know that his is a habit with probable results. Likewise, a simple numerological character analysis may show tendencies in a person that will have consequences in the future, even if we cannot say when.

Second, knowing someone's name — even a single nickname — helps us evaluate the person. Let us say that you go by the nickname of BOB and you have struck up a casual conversation with a man who goes by the name of PETE, whose surname you do not yet know. You have met at a tavern, you seem to have a lot of interests in common, and he seems to present the possibility of a real friendship, so now, before you even know him well enough to get his full name, you make a quick numerological character sketch, similar in depth to that provided by Sun Sign Astrology:

PETE	BOB
7 5 2 5	2 6 2
19	10
1	**1**

No wonder the two of you hit it off so well! You both prefer to be known by a short nickname, and both of your nicknames work out to the identical masculine, adventurous, do-and-dare number 1. This man speaks your language and you speak his, and so he may become your buddy in time.

You can do a deeper analysis later, when you get to know his full name, but for now, the road is open and the lights are green.

CHARACTER ANALYSIS OF THE NAME AS PRESENTED

Assessing the degree of compatibility between yourself and another person is not the only reason to craft a numerical character analysis. Another reason, which finds particular value in schools and businesses, is to assist in treating each person with compassion. For example, we are wiser helpers when we understand what self-presentation is when hiring someone for a job or mediating between two people at a school or job site.

For this purpose, we will use the name exactly as it is presented — that is, without an attempt to uncover the true birth name, the current legal name, or the birth date. In fact, we are directly assessing the character-impression the person brings to the social situation in which we meet.

Let us take as an example a man named CHUCK OWEN. This is the name on his business card and in the telephone directory. For our present purposes it does not matter whether his full birth name is CHARLES DANIEL OWEN or CHARLEMAGNE JOHNSON JONES — to us he is clearly and simply CHUCK OWEN. We have known him thus for many years, and as such he has built his reputation with our business.

So who is he "being" for us? How is he presenting himself? Let's see:

$$
\begin{array}{cc}
\textbf{C H U C K} & \textbf{O W E N} \\
3\ 8\ 3\ 3\ 2 & 6\ 5\ 5\ 5 \\
19 & 21 \\
1 & 3 \\
\multicolumn{2}{c}{\textbf{4}}
\end{array}
$$

He presents as a physical worker, an outdoorsman, and a collector with a bent for practical science and hard labour. We shall not offer him a desk job in quiet solitude, as we might if we knew that his birth name was:

$$
\begin{array}{ccc}
\textbf{C H E S T E R} & \textbf{D A V O E} & \textbf{O W E N S F O R T H} \\
3\ 8\ 5\ 1\ 2\ 5\ 9 & 4\ 1\ 4\ 6\ 5 & 6\ 5\ 5\ 5\ 1\ 6\ 6\ 9\ 2\ 8 \\
33 & 20 & 53 \\
6 & 2 & 8 \\
\multicolumn{3}{c}{\textbf{7}}
\end{array}
$$

Not every contemplative 7 becomes a rugged 4. but this man has.

THE FIRST NAME OR VITAL NUMBER

This is also called the Given Name Number, and it is made from the number of your first name. In most cases, it was chosen for you at birth, and unless you change it, this name remains close to you all your life.

THE SURNAME OR HEREDITARY NUMBER

This is the number of your surname or family. Women may change this upon marriage, but it still holds the power of the father's lineage.

THE FULL BIRTH NAME OR DESTINY NUMBER

The number worked out by analyzing the full name at birth, also called the Distinguishing or Destiny Number, is greatly valued because its vibration governs the individual more than any other number. This is obtained by adding all the letters in the full name given at birth, with middle name or names included.

Consciously or unconsciously, this number directs and affects us, even when we cast it off, hide it, or leave it behind in favour of a nickname, initials, a married name, or a professional pseudonym. It makes no difference if an individual has never used the birth name or dislikes it, or prefers to be called by some other name, the full birth name number is the the number of true soul self-analysis, and it is widely said that it is more important to know our own Destiny Number than any other one number connected to ourselves.

```
M A R Y   J A N E   F R E E M A N
4 1 9 7   1 1 5 5   6 9 5 5 4 1 5
  21        12          35
  3         3           8
            14
            5
```

MARY is **3**, the Vital Number. JANE is also **3**. FREEMAN is **8**, the Hereditary Number. The sum of 3 plus 3 plus 8 = 14, and then 1 plus 4 = **5**. Therefore MARY JANE FREEMAN's Destiny Number is **5**.

CONSONANTS ONLY: THE APPEARANCE NUMBER

The consonants form the hard outer shell of language. The Appearance Number or Persona Number is the name written only with consonants. It tells how a person wishes to be perceived. If harmonious to the Destiny Number (full name) and the Heart's Desire Number (vowels only), all is well; if it is significantly inharmonious, the person presents a "false front" to the world.

```
M   A   R   Y    J   A   N   E    F   R   E   E   M   A   N
4 - 9 - 1 - 5  - 6   9 - - - 4 - 5
        13           6              24
                     43
                      7
```

VOWELS ONLY: THE HEART'S DESIRE NUMBER

The Heart's Desire, sometimes called the Soul Number, is the single digit sum of the vowels of the name, excluding consonants. A number of inner feeling, it tells how we desire to express our destiny. MARY JANE FREEMAN's Destiny Number is **5.** Her Appearance Number is **7.** Now we shall count the vowels in her birth name. The final Y in MARY is sounded as a vowel ("ee") and counts as such. Were her surname YOUNGER, the initial Y, not sounded as a vowel, would not be counted as such.

```
M   A   R   Y    J   A   N   E    F   R   E   E   M   A   N
  - 1 - 7 -    - 1 - 5  - - - 5   5 - - 1 -
        8            6              11
                     25
                      7
```

MARY JANE FREEMAN's Destiny Number of **5** brings adjustment to life's uncertainties through non-resistance, but now we see that she will choose to express this as a **7,** both outwardly in the Persona Number and inwardly through her Heart's Desire for quiet retreat and solitary meditation. The Destiny Number tells the life's lesson, the Persona indicates how she appears to us, and the Heart's Desire is her chosen manner of expression.

SUMMARY OF THE DESTINY NUMBERS

- **Destiny Number 1:** You will learn to express true individuality, not by dominance, but through success, building unity and understanding.
- **Destiny Number 2:** You will develop a sense of fairness and justice and will at all times be the peacemaker or the diplomat.
- **Destiny Number 3:** You will bring joy to all people through the active and radiant expressive power within your life.
- **Destiny Number 4:** You will gain true soul experience through endeavour and hard work, and your labour will bring financial returns.
- **Destiny Number 5:** You will learn that uncertainty is all around us, but non-resistance brings harmonious adjustment to external changes.
- **Destiny Number 6:** You will give up much in humanitarian service for others, and you may express yourself though musical talent.
- **Destiny Number 7:** You will see the occult meaning of all things, and although you prefer solitude, you will be sought out for your insight.
- **Destiny Number 8:** You will learn much through the experiences, trials, and pleasures that come from mastery of the financial world.
- **Destiny Number 9:** You will learn that all life is one, and at all times will strive to express universal love and compassion.
- **Destiny Number 11:** You will find a life of empathic healing service through your gifted spiritual and material intelligence and wisdom.
- **Destiny Number 22:** You will learn to use your practical skills in the service of large and visionary undertakings for the good of many.
- **Destiny Number 33:** You will become a guide to those who are seeking to understand cosmic principles as they traverse their lives.

Here are three examples of how a Destiny Number of 4 — the practical, stable, hard-worker with scientific interests who may in time acquire wealth — expresses itself through varying Heart's Desires:

- **Destiny 4 and Heart's Desire 1:** Keen desire for leadership in the financial and practical world; may become a real estate developer.
- **Destiny 4 and Heart's Desire 5:** One who works to accumulate money or land for social success while moving from place to place.
- **Destiny 4 and Heart's Desire 7:** A mechanical inventor, student, or scientist who makes no great outward show of his activities.

CHAPTER SIX
INTERPRETING THE BIRTH DATE NUMBER

THE BIRTH DATE OR LIFE PATH NUMBER

The Birth Date Number, often called the Life Path Number, is the digit that results when the day, month, and year of birth are added. For example:

March 23, 1924 is **3-2-3-1-9-2-4.** This sums to 24, and 2 plus 4 = **6.**

Having learned to apply numbers to a person's birth date and to reduce it, what now remains is to interpret it. Let us say that your birth date reduces to a 6, as above. You can, of course, consult the pages on the characters of the numbers and learn the meaning of the 6, but what is needed first is a full understanding of what the birth number actually means to a person.

When a soul comes onto this planet, it comes to take up a lesson, and this lesson is told by the distinguishing birth name or Destiny Number, which is the complete sum of the letters of the name given at birth. The power behind the life and in the soul for working out this new lesson, and the force with which it comes forth, is told by the birth date number.

This important number is the record of how we entered into life; it tells of our gifts, our strength, our latent force, our subjective knowledge and understanding, and the power we have behind us for working out the lessons of life's experiences. It is our passport for entrance into Earth life; it shows what the soul has to its credit and what it has already included before contacting the experiences of this time on Earth. Whether you consider it to be a token of God's gifts, the lessons learned in past lives, or the measure of your genetic heritage, the Life Path represents innate knowledge and inclinations which we bring into life at the time of birth.

Like Numerology, Astrology also tells us, by means of the natal horoscope, unique information about our birth date, giving an account of our native abilities and gifts. The Life Path Number is Numerology's equivalent to Astrology's natal horoscope. How each individual understands the natal chart or the numerological Birth Date Number will vary of course, but it is a fact that when betting, the most common lucky number people choose is not the full name or Destiny Number, but rather the humble birth date. It holds a power that cannot be denied.

VOCATIONAL NUMBER: LIFE PATH PLUS DESTINY

To understand the meaning of the Life Path number, you may simply return to the chapter on the character of the numbers. However, for a more detailed look into the interplay between the Birth Date and the Full Birth Name, it is customary to add the two and then reduce them in the usual way. In this manner we arrive at a new number, called the Vocational Number. It is called that because it indicates the general kind of job, career, or profession best suited for the person. Imparting this information to a child may provide valuable occupational guidance from a young age.

Those with odd Vocational Numbers work best alone or as leaders, and those with even Vocational Numbers work best in association with others.

- **Vocational Number 1:** Professional, military, or public leadership is indicated; analytical abilities may lead to a career as a critic or editor.
- **Vocational Number 2:** A peaceful career in justice, peacemaking, social work, mediation, or diplomacy is suggested, as is homemaking.
- **Vocational Number 3:** A career in the arts, on stage, or as a promoter of artistic, musical, or dance events would be a natural choice for you.
- **Vocational Number 4:** Skilled trades, agriculture, or basic scientific research in field or laboratory will reward your capacity for hard work.
- **Vocational Number 5:** Your quick mind enables you to enjoy several entirely different career paths in life, as you adjust to external changes.
- **Vocational Number 6:** Public affairs, support for social progress, and being of humanitarian service will satisfy your intellect and your heart.
- **Vocational Number 7:** A conventional career in the professions or business may not suit your meditative and introspective inclinations.
- **Vocational Number 8:** Business at any scale, from a small shop to a large corporation or a financial investment firm, will probably appeal.
- **Vocational Number 9:** You will have more choices in career than most, and will select one that is artistic, virtuous, and long-abiding.
- **Vocational Number 11:** You may embark on a career as an empathic healer, spiritual medium, intuitive psychic, or wisdom teacher.
- **Vocational Number 22:** You may become a theoretician or practical planner of large-scale, forward-looking cooperative undertakings.
- **Vocational Number 33:** You will probably not seek out a typical career, but you will be sought out as a guide by sincere students.

CHAPTER SEVEN
HOW TO FIND YOUR PLACE OF POWER

While the Vocational Number is probably the most popular way to indicate a suitable occupation, a different numerical technique, called the Four Planes Method, has also found its proponents and devotees.

THE FOUR PLANES METHOD

Everyone has a natural place of power from which to radiate attraction for success and accomplishment. When this place is found and recognized, the current of life flows with the individual, helping and assisting all efforts, and the living of life becomes comfortable, easy, and successful instead of an existence full of hardships, difficulties, and resistance.

There are four planes of being within every individual, each plane having its own characteristics and manner of expression. These planes of being are called physical, mental, emotional, and intuitive. Every soul or individual functions principally from one or two of these planes, or from all, according to the arrangement of the numbers of the name.

We first write out each of the names comprising the full name, letter by letter, including all middle names, and assign each letter to one of the four planes. Then we total up the number of occurrences of each number according to its plane. Finally, we note as a modifier the Destiny Number, which is taken into consideration when choosing the occupation.

If the four planes are developed in almost equal balance, this gives a well-rounded person who can contact life at any point or place and always command a good measure of success. However, most people will have one or two of the four planes predominating over the others.

NUMERICAL ANALYSIS OF THE FOUR PLANES

The numbers, according to this Four Planes division, are as follows:

- **The Mental Plane numbers are 1 and 8.**
- **The Emotional Plane numbers are 2 and 3 and 6.**
- **The Intuitive Plane numbers are 7 and 9.**
- **The Physical Plane numbers are 4 and 5.**

THE MENTAL PLANE

The mental plane is the reasoning plane and gives fine logic and deduction, analysis, order, arrangement and a desire for proof and facts. This is the plane in which self-direction and initiative occur and it is also the plane that gives real business ability, or power for financial success in the world where reason rules.

• **The Mental Plane numbers in a name are 1 and 8.**

THE EMOTIONAL PLANE

The emotional plane is the plane of impulse: here reason is not found and ideals take its place. When emotional characteristics prevail, we have an individual governed by imagination and feelings, and because of this power for deep feeling, this plane is called the artistic plane and as a rule gives ability or expression in some artistic direction.

• **The Emotional Plane numbers in a name are 2 and 3 and 6.**

THE INTUITIVE PLANE

The intuitive plane is the plane of direct inspiration, and gives ability to know and understand without proof, reason, or even feeling, because something deep within it guides it at all times. When a name shows many intuitive numbers, we know that the intuition can be trusted. This is a religious plane and gives high spirituality.

• **The Intuitive Plane numbers in a name are 7 and 9.**

THE PHYSICAL PLANE

The physical plane gives the characteristics which we call practical: a desire for creature comforts and a generally steady disposition. This plane is governed by what is known as natural instinct. When physical numbers are many, there is usually a tendency to pursue the rational and the scientific and not much interest in things idealistic or spiritual.

• **The Physical Plane numbers in a name are 4 and 5.**

OCCUPATIONS AS TOLD BY THE FOUR PLANE METHOD

When analyzed as described, by enumerating all of the letters and assigning each number to its designated plane, most occupational readings will not show one single plane predominating, nor will it show an even distribution of all four planes. Therefore, here are some commonly seen combinations, and their places of power.

Physical 4 or 5 plus Mental 1 or 8: If a name has more physical and mental numbers, the place of power is in the business world of mercantile concerns, buying and selling, figuring and scheming, and in a smaller way, working as stenographers, clerks, and store keepers.

Emotional 2 or 3 or 6 plus Physical 4 or 5: If there are more emotional and physical numbers, the place of power is in the artistic business world of interior decorators, gardeners, or in any line of artistic work that leads with emotions, backed by order, arrangement, and analysis.

Intuitive 7 and 9 plus Physical 4 or 5: If the physical and intuitive characteristics are strongest, we find people who are a little out of the ordinary. Sometimes they are evangelists, sometimes humanitarians, lecturers, or teachers. They usually have a great ability to influence others.

Mental 1 or 8 Plus Emotional 2 or 3 or 6: If there are more mental and emotional numbers, the place of power is an occupation where mind and cleverness are harnessed to the heart. Here we see writers of musical comedy, advertisements, and those who sell sentimental art.

Mental 1 or 8 plus Intuitive 7 and 9: If there are more mental and intuitive numbers, the place of power for life is in the specialized world of surgeons, dentists, lawyers, traveling salesmen, or in any way that reason rules, yet allows some play to the imagination.

Emotional 2 or 3 or 6 plus Intuitive 7 and 9: If the emotional and intuitive numbers predominate, then the place for greatest success, both for money and happiness, is in the purely artistic world, as musicians, composers, dancer, actors, artists, and sculptors.

OCCUPATIONAL ANALYSIS BY THE PLANES

Let us now apply the Four Planes technique to guiding a person who seeks information about a suitable occupation.

JOSEPHINE   ANABEL   SCOTT
1 6 1 5 7 8 9 5 5   1 5 1 2 5 3   1 3 6 2 2 (= 78)

Physical numbers (4 and 5) occur 5 times.
Mental numbers (1 and 8) occur 6 times. } **Predominating**
Emotional numbers (2, 3, 6) occur 7 times. } **Planes**
Intuitive numbers (7 and 9) occur 2 times.
Destiny Number 78 is 7 plus 8 = 15; 15 is 1 plus 5 = **6.**

The Mental and Emotional Planes predominate, so here we have an artistic business woman, one whose place of power is in the mercantile world but not in the areas of analysis, acquisition, and fact, rather in an occupation where there would be a chance for her to develop a commercial expression of her fine artistic imagination and sincere feelings.

Her Mental numbers consist of five 1s and one 8, indicating a desire to be a innovative leader (1), but not one who enters the business world to "win" or to accumulate great wealth (8).

Her Emotional Plane numbers consist of three 2s, two 3s, and two 6s. With 2 leading the pack, so to speak, she has a lovely feminine quality which is gentle and nurturing.

Finally, her Destiny Number is 6, which is the great humanitarian, altruistic, and musical number associated with teaching, nursing, and with matrons or directors in hospitals or charity organizations. This works well with the two 6s in her predominating Emotional Plane.

Therefore, she would probably find happiness and success in teaching music or art to the young. She might also excel as the owner and chief designer of a small millinery or fine clothing shop, employing a few talented women whose lives she would uplift. In sum, she is suitable to any occupation that gives artistic service to others, brings her recognition, and requires of her a good business head, keen judgement, and a kind heart.

If her birth number is a 1 (say, May 2, 1911) she will incline more to the financial side; if a 2 (say, May 3, 1911), she will emphasize her artistry.

CHAPTER EIGHT
BIRTH DATE NUMEROLOGY
AND THE MAGIC SQUARE

Magic Squares are number grids with an unusual property. If you add the numbers in them by column, by row, or on the diagonals, the sum will always be the same. Mathematicians delight in creating new Magic Squares, but only one form is used in Numerology — and it is ancient.

In China, the 3 x 3 Magic Square grid, in which all of the columns, rows, and diagonals sum up to 15, has long been known as the Lo Shu Square or Scroll of the River Lo. The tale is told that the numerals that comprised the array were first observed by the Emperor Yu on the shell of a gigantic Tortoise who emerged from the river. This numerical pattern was said to embody great spiritual truths, and in time it gave rise to the Ba Gua or Eight Trigram Diagram of the Universe, and thence to the 64 hexagrams of the I Ching system of divination, as well as forming the basis for the famous Flying Star School of Feng Shui.

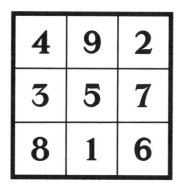 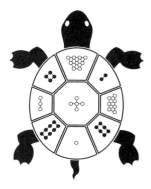

Meanwhile, in the ancient Middle East and Europe, seven different Magic Squares were assigned to the Seven Sacred Planets that ruled the seven days of the week — the Sun, Moon, Mars, Mercury, Jupiter, Venus, and Saturn. The Square of Saturn is identical with the Lo Shu Square.

Saturn, the most distant planet visable to the naked eye, is associated with time and our future fates, and thus the Saturn Square has deep meaning to Western diviners, just as the Lo Shu Square does in Asia.

THE LO SHU OR SATURN SQUARE IS NOT THE 123 GRID

Before describing how to employ the Magic Square of Saturn in Numerology, it is necessary to distinguish it from a similar-looking tic-tac-toe layout that is known as the 123 Grid, the Name Diagram, the Number Grid, the Vitruvian Square, Karmic Numerology, and, sometimes, quite wrongfully, the Simplified or Simple Lo Shu Square. It is that latter name that causes the confusion, so let's take a look.

In the Magic or Lo Shu square at left, ALL the columns, rows, and diagonals "magically" sum to 15, while in the 123 Grid, they do NOT:

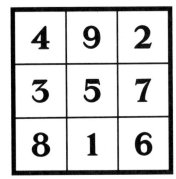 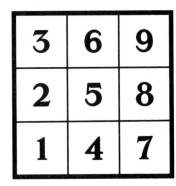

We will work only with the true Square of Saturn or Lo Shu Square, in which all rows, columns, and diagonals sum up to 15. The approach will be Chinese, but adapted to the Gregorian-solar civil calendar.

(To learn culturally traditional Lo Shu numerology as performed with the Chinese lunar calendar, the works of Lillian Too are recommended. Additionally, some Western authors, including Dennis Perez, Scott Grossberg, and Norman Shine, teach how to read the 123 Grid for date or name numbers, and you may also find their books of interest.)

3-6-9-15-45: HIDDEN NUMBERS IN THE MAGIC SQUARE

- Each row, column, and diagonal contains **3** number-spaces.
- All rows, columns, and diagonals sum to **15** and 15 reduces to **6**.
- The square contains **9** numbers total.
- All the numbers in the entire square sum to **45** and 45 reduces to **9**.

YIN AND YANG IN THE MAGIC SQUARE

The Magic Square is used to obtain a numerological character reading from a birth date or to make a prediction for any date. The method described here, while not purely Chinese, derives from the basic concepts of Chinese Lo Shu Square Numerology as popularized for English-speakers.

The numbers have different meanings in Asia than in the West, and these will be explained below. The visual patterns formed by the numbers are also essential to reading the square, and so that is where we will start.

In both Asian and Western numerology, the even numbers **2-4-6-8** are considered feminine, receptive, or yin, while the odd numbers **1-3-5-7-9** are masculine, active, or yang. Notice their placement on the Lo Shu Square:

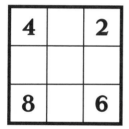
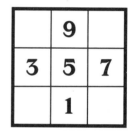

PUTTING A BIRTH DATE IN THE SQUARE

For our first example, let us take the birth date February 15, 1928, rendered in numbers as 2-15-1928. All zeroes will be ignored, as there is no place for them, so now we have only **2-1-5-1-9-2-8.** These are put in their assigned spaces within the Magic Square. Duplicates or triplicates of the same number go into the same assigned space, separated by commas.

This is what February 15, 1928 looks like in the Magic Square:

	9	2,2
	5	
8	1,1	

PRACTICE FILLING IN THE SQUARES WITH DATES

At this point, it is a good idea to make a few empty grids for yourself. Use three or four of your grids to put in the birth dates of your friends and family. Practice until placing the numbers becomes easy.

NOTICE THE POSITIVE LINES AND NEGATIVE ARROWS

Just as in tic-tac-toe, a line is drawn to mark three consecutive boxes with the same content. We will look for **NUMBERED BOXES** versus **BLANK BOXES.** Here is the birth date April 8, 1921, or **4-8-1-9-2-1:**

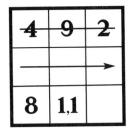

The top row, in which the numbers **4-9-2** fill all three spaces, is marked by a "positive line," as if you have won it in tic-tac-toe.

The second row, consisting of three blank squares in which no date numbers appear, contains a "negative arrow." In Chinese thinking, arrows have the potential for harm and are read as less than optimal energies.

Both positive lines and negative arrows can run horizontally along the rows, vertically down the columns, or diagonally, from corner to corner.

Here is a sample for the birth date August 23, 1932 or **8-2-3-1-9-3-2.** In this example, a negative arrow runs diagonally from corner to corner.

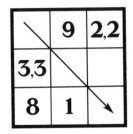

A SQUARE MAY CONTAIN MULTIPLE LINES AND ARROWS

Quite often a square will have more than one filled or blank line or arrow. When this happens, all of the lines and arrows are read.

The birth date April 25, 1937 or **4-2-5-1-9-3-7** has three positive lines; top horizontal row, middle horizontal row, and middle vertical column:

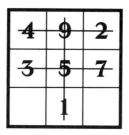

July 3, 1937 or **7-3-1-9-3-7** contains two diagonal negative arrows:

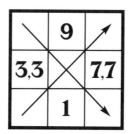

A SQUARE MAY CONTAIN NO LINES OR ARROWS AT ALL

The birth date August 4, 1917 or **8-4-1-9-1-7** makes neither positive lines nor negative arrows: All of the numbers are "loose."

CHAPTER NINE
READING LO SHU LINES AND ARROWS

A KEY TO THE PATTERNS

Each horizontal row, vertical column, and corner-to-corner diagonal is said to govern a general area of life. The sixteen patterns of positive lines (filled spaces) and negative arrows (blank spaces) in these rows, columns, and diagonals form the basis for the numerological reading.

In the pages that follow, a detailed character analysis will be given for each line and arrow pattern. Before delving into them, note that the eight positive lines (the rows, columns, and diagonals with three filled spaces) are generally more positive in interpretation than the eight arrows (the rows, columns, and diagonals with three blank spaces).

	Positive (Filled) Line	Negative (Empty) Arrow
Horizontal		
4 9 2	Intellect, Intelligence	Memory, Learn by Doing
3 5 7	Calmness, Spirituality	Sensitivity, Loneliness
8 1 6	Practicality, Prosperity	Abstract Ideas, Philosophy
Vertical		
4 3 8	Planning, Shrewdness	Envisioning, Confusion
9 5 1	Self-Assurance, Will	Self-Doubt, Vacillation
2 7 6	Action, Activity	Contemplation, Apathy
Diagonal		
4 5 6	Belief, Faith, Serenity	Disbelief, Skepticism
8 5 2	Advance, Determination	Retreat, Frustration

Either Many Lines or Many Arrows
                     Blended Positive Traits   Blended Negative Traits

A Blend of Both Lines and Arrows
                     A Complex Personality

Neither Lines Nor Arrows
                     A Cryptic and Unfulfilled Personality

THE LINE OF INTELLECT: NUMBERS IN 4-9-2

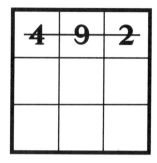

A positive line running through the top row brings intelligence, clear thought, intellectuality, and the ability to apply logic to problems. Because technical interests run higher than feelings, the person may receive an unjust reputation as cold and uncaring, but self-training in social contact will allow the true heart's natural warmth to shine. A career in academia, basic research, or the judiciary will bring success.

THE ARROW OF MEMORY: BLANKS IN 4-9-2

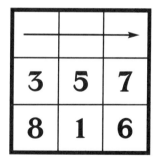

A negative arrow running through the top row places an emphasis on memory as the conveyance of acquired knowledge. The person learns by doing, by repetition, and by forming clear memories of what has been done in the past. In order to succeed, it is important for those born with this pattern to avoid distractions, to pay attention to established procedures and techniques, and to finish tasks once begun.

THE LINE OF CALM BALANCE: NUMBERS IN 3-5-7

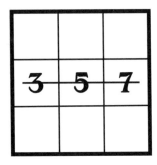

A positive line running through the middle row brings emotional poise, a calm approach to life's ups and downs, and the ability to weigh the balance between logic and feelings. People with this configuration are sought out as friends and are respected by those above and below them in status, because they are fair and filled with faith. Not only are they emotionally balanced, they can convey peace to those around them.

THE ARROW OF SENSITIVITY: BLANKS IN 3-5-7

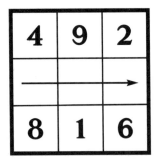

A negative arrow running through the middle row indicates a person who is sensitive, loyal, tender-hearted, and given to deep feelings that are easily engaged and openly displayed. Quick to detect and respond to emotional influences projected by friends, family, and even strangers, this person is easily hurt by harsh comments or verbal cruelty, but can develop self-control so as not to fall prey to self-pity and loneliness.

THE LINE OF PRACTICALITY: NUMBERS IN 8-1-6

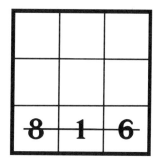

A positive line running through the bottom row is a sign of effective practical skills expressed in a straightforward manner, with an emphasis on getting things done. Because constructive talent with the hands coupled with artistic creativity can be used to earn a good living, this is a line of prosperity and monetary fortune. Some may say that this person is materialistic and worldly, but such is rarely the case.

THE ARROW OF ABSTRACT IDEAS: BLANKS IN 8-1-6

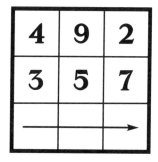

A negative arrow running through the bottom row brings a form of philosophical abstraction in which theoretical concepts are grasped and understood, but practical follow-through activity is lacking. There is little interest in wealth or material goods. Although the principles of science, politics, economics, and religion are of great interest to this person, such studies should not be allowed to eclipse the mundane needs of daily life.

THE LINE OF THE PLANNER: NUMBERS IN 4-3-8

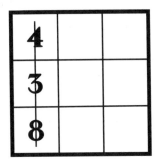

A positive line running through the left column is a sign of the capacity to plan projects and events. A person of this type is organized and efficient. The tendency to think ahead may be coupled with the ability to make estimates for materials or labour needed for projects, and those who can plan well for others are always in demand in managerial roles. This line may also bring political success or corporate work.

THE ARROW OF THE ENVISIONER: BLANKS IN 4-3-8

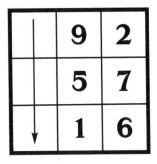

A negative arrow running through the left column indicates a strong fantasy life, in which vivid images and thoughts hold sway. The person may become so absorbed in these visions as to forget routine tasks. If expression is added to imagination, then art, poetry, and music may result; but without an expressive outlet, the person becomes confused and makes no success in the world, despite the wealth of inner ideation.

THE LINE OF SELF-ASSURANCE: NUMBERS IN 9-5-1

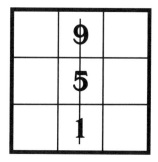

A positive line running through the middle column brings strong self-confidence and will power. It greatly increases the person's energy, due to innate self-assurance and feelings of self-worth. However, those who believe they always know the right way to proceed and who bossily tell others what to do may be perceived as pushy or domineering; they should take time to listen to colleagues and followers.

THE ARROW OF SELF-DOUBT: BLANKS IN 9-5-1

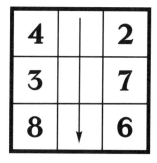

A negative arrow running through the middle column is associated with frustration that springs from high self-expectations, as well as expectations concerning family and colleagues. When this person meets with difficulty in achievement, the tendency for self-blame and regret can be crippling, but learning to accept that progress sometimes comes more slowly than desired will in time calm self-doubt.

THE LINE OF ACTION: NUMBERS IN 2-7-6

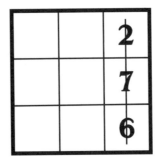

A positive line running through the right column brings high energy and much activity in life. Starting new projects is almost a passion, and if the Arrow of Determination (the diagonal 8-5-2) is found, the person may actually verge on hyperactivity. The only drawback to this line is the possibility of the person starting too many enthusiastic projects in too short a time, and then leaving others to come behind and finish them.

THE ARROW OF CONTEMPLATION: BLANKS IN 2-7-6

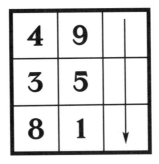

A negative arrow running through the right column is associated with passivity. The person is by no means lazy, but has a hard time "getting off the starting line," and spends much time in contemplation of upcoming projects without actually beginning the work. This person can use some help getting started. However, if the Line of Self-Assurance (9-5-1) is found, a slow start leads to a great outcome.

THE LINE OF BELIEF: NUMBERS IN 4-5-6

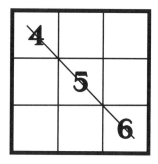

A positive line running from corner to corner, upper left to lower right, is an indication of innate spirituality and deep abiding faith. The person may or may not belong to any particular organized religion but, regardless of adherence or attendance in church or temple, will live a life that bears witness to an inner experience of true contact with the realm of Spirit, Deity, or the Universe, however such is conceived.

THE ARROW OF SKEPTICISM: BLANKS IN 4-5-6

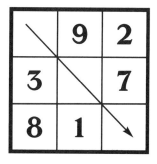

A negative arrow running from corner to corner, upper left to lower right, is associated with a questioning nature and a disinclination to accept any information unless it is proven to the person's own satisfaction. In time the person may become cynical or suspicious of the motives of others. Another difficulty with the refusal of belief arises when skepticism itself becomes a form of dogma, leaving the person bereft of faith or trust.

THE LINE OF DETERMINATION: NUMBERS IN 8-5-2

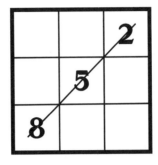

A positive line running from corner to corner, lower left to upper right, brings positive power, fortitude, and indomitable determination. The person forges on despite difficulties, patiently persists in the face of adversity, endures all setbacks, comes back stronger than ever, never takes "no" for an answer, and, driven by pride as much as confidence, will stick with a project until it is finished or worry at a problem until it solved.

THE ARROW OF CONTEMPLATION: BLANKS IN 8-5-2

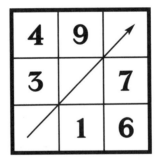

A negative arrow running from corner to corner, lower left to upper right, is associated with a person who is contemplative, and much given to considering the ways of the world. When this person's plans are opposed, retreat is likely, often under the guise of putting the welfare of others before that of the self. Frustration with the stressful ways of the world may lead this person to prefer meditation and quiet observation to bold action.

NO LINES OR ARROWS AT ALL

4		**2**
		7
8	**1**	

A person whose date comes out with NO lines and NO arrows at all is in a cryptic position, much like a person with unaspected planets in Astrology. In order to accomplish much or to find luck, the person is advised to bond with a mate whose numbers complete the missing patterns, forming positive lines in order to share in the luck and life of the partner. In the above example, a mate with both **4-9-2** and **4-3-8** would help, but far better would be a mate with a **6.**

A MULTIPLICITY OF BLANK ARROWS

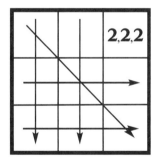

On rare dates, only one or two numbers appear and the chart is marked by a multiplicity of blank (unfilled) arrows. An extreme example of this is February 2, 2000 **(2-2-2)**. This person's five blank arrows are Sensitivity **(3-5-7)**, Abstract Ideas **(8-1-6)**, Envisioning **(4-3-8)**, Self-Doubt **(9-5-1)**, and Disbelief **(4-5-6)**; a difficult combination, to say the least. Companions with **4-9-2, 2-7-6,** or **8-5-2**, who link to the isolated 2s, will be of help.

CHAPTER TEN
THE MEANING OF THE LO SHU NUMBERS

- **Number 1** is associated with speech and hearing, expressive verbal communication, the ability to converse honestly, and the capacity to listen to others. When negative, it is over-talkative.

- **Number 2** is associated with emotional sensitivity, fine intuitive insights, and psychic abilities. When negative, it is over-sensitive to outside stimuli and thus prone to reclusive behaviour.

- **Number 3** is associated with intellectual capacity, logic, memory, planning, and the ability to solve problems. When negative, the imagination gives rise to plans and fantasies that cannot be realized.

- **Number 4** is associated with self-control, orderliness, pragmatism, neatness, practicality, and a willingness to take on hard work. When negative, it is merely physical and does not aspire to greater heights.

- **Number 5** is associated with emotional calm, mental balance, stability, steadiness, persistence, and freedom from rigid thought. When negative, it is so quick-acting that it may become impulsive.

- **Number 6** is associated with creativity, helpfulness, love, and caring for the home, children, family, and friends. When negative, it can become insecure or fearful about the home and the children.

- **Number 7** is associated with disappointment and sacrifice in love, health, and money, learning through experience and through loss. When negative, the sacrifices are so great that suffering results.

- **Number 8** is associated with discipline, organization, scrupulous dealings, attention to detail, and demandingly high goals. When negative, it is obsessive, materialistic, and ceaselessly acquisitive.

- **Number 9** is associated with intelligence, idealism, humanitarian beliefs, and the courage to inspire change for the common good. When negative, it withdraws its brilliance and becomes a loner.

KEY TO THE REPETITION OF NUMBERS IN THE SQUARE

Tracking and recording the number of times a numeral appears in a birth date is an important Lo Shu Numerology method not found in the "reducing" forms of Numerology traditional in Europe and the Americas. The number of repetitions of a numeral has a meaning in keeping with Asian philosophical concepts that place a value on "the great middle." In Europe and America, this is called "The Goldilocks Principle," after the folkloric Grimm's fairy tale of *Goldilocks and the Three Bears,* in which the little girl Goldilocks repeatedly rejects items that are too small or too big, too hot or too cold, and declares "just right" only those things in the mid-range of her experiences. In Lo Shu Numerology, the meanings of the numerals undergo a subtle shift as they move from one occurrence to two, three, four, or more. Once is good, twice is a refinement, three times signifies over-ripeness, and four times or more is degenerative.

Here is a condensed table describing the effect of numerical repetition. Because the theory is obvious, in time it will become second nature to you.

	One Time	*Two Times*	*Three Times*	*Four Times*
1	Quiet Speech	Honest Speech	Talkativeness	Over-Sharing
2	Sensitive	Intuitive	Over-Sensitive	Reclusive
3	Talented	Creative	Imaginative	Fantasy-Prone
4	Orderly	Pragmatic	Hard Working	Materialistic
5	Stable	Enthusiastic	Energetic	Frenetic
6	Helpful	Caring	Emotional	Fearful
7	Empirical	Spiritual	Stoical	Suffering
8	Organized	Scrupulous	Demanding	Obsessive
9	Intelligent	Idealistic	Humanitarian	Eccentric

DATES MAY SHARE THE SAME LO SHU PATTERN

Just as many dates reduce to the same number in Western Numerology, so do many dates display the same arrow pattern in their Lo Shu Squares.

For example, April 17, 1925 (**4-1-7-1-9-2-5**) has the same pattern as May 12, 1947 (**5-1-2-1-9-4-7**): both are Self-Assured, Honest Intellectuals.

Likewise, January 15, 1926 (**1-1-5-1-9-2-6**) has the pattern of October 25, 1961 (**1-0-2-5-1-9-6-1**): both are Self-Assured, Talkative Dreamers.

AN ASIDE FOR STATISTICIANS: MATH FUN BREAK!

By now the statisticians among us will have noticed that Magic Square Numerology is not sortilege, and that the strict calendrical restraints placed on the numbers that fill the squares preclude an easily ascertained cyclical pattern of simple, rapidly repeated values.

For instance, every person born in the 19th century will have a 1 and an 8 in his array, every person born in the 20th century will have a 1 and a 9 in his array, and every person born in the 21st century will have a 2 (but not a 0, because there are no zeroes) in his array.

Some numerologists may discount this by saying, "If everybody has at least one 1 and one 8 (or one 1 and one 9, or one 2), those are trivial and should not be read," but a better way to handle it is by analogy to the "generational aspects" made by the ultra-slow-moving planets in Astrology.

In this case, each "generation" lasts one full century. The 19th century, with its 1s of communication and 8s of organization, and the 20th century with its 1s of communication and its 9s of idealism, will give way to the 21st century, where the 2s will emphasize emotional sensitivity.

After discarding zeroes, it is obvious that every date in our modern calendar produces from three to eight digits, with or without repetition:

March 1, 2000	**(3-1-2)**
February 2, 2002	**(2-2-2-2)**
March 30, 1910	**(3-3-1-9-1)**
January 7, 1934	**(1-7-1-9-3-4)**
June 12, 1915	**(6-1-2-1-9-1-5)**
December 31, 1944	**(1-2-3-1-1-9-4-4)**

Because about two-thirds of the dates in each month have two digits and most 20th century years lack a zero, a seven-digit array is the most common 20th century pattern — but the 21st century has an obligatory zero in every year, producing a "generation" among whom six digits is more common.

A "mathematical sieve" for Lo Shu Squares must take into account the constraints of month-length and the discard of zeroes, but even without a formal sieve, it appears that birth dates with high repetitions and few digits are likely to produce both arrows and "loose numbers" and that people born in November and December will have more repetitions of the digits 1 or 2.

CHAPTER ELEVEN
READING THE LO SHU SQUARE

COMBINING NUMBERS, LINES, AND ARROWS

We have now learned the 36 rules of Lo Shu Square Numerology:

- **18 Number Meanings**
  - 9 Basic Number Meanings
  - 9 Shifts in Number Meanings Due to Repetition
- **18 Pattern Meanings**
  - 8 Positive Line Patterns
  - 8 Negative Arrow Patterns
  - 1 "No Pattern"
  - 1 "Multiple Blanks" Pattern

We can now put these elements together and deliver a full reading. Three examples will bring the method into clear focus. After studying them, you will be ready to unfold the meaning of your own Magic Square.

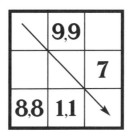

Example One: The birth date is July 18, 1989 or **7-1-8-1-9-8-9.**

This is a highly intelligent person whose intellect inclines toward idealism and high expectations (two 9s). Extremely self-disciplined, and organized to the point of scrupulosity (two 8s), this person is an honest communicator, but may be perceived as a bit too blunt (two 1s). Having suffered losses because others are not always intelligent, orderly, or honest, this person takes an empirical rather than a hopeful viewpoint to avoid further disappointments (one 7). The result is a stance of cynical skepticism, with no faith in the innate goodness of the Universe (arrow 4-5-6).

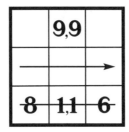

Example Two. The birth date is January 8th, 1996 or **1-8-1-9-9-6.**

This is another highly intelligent person whose intellect inclines toward idealism and high expectations (two 9s). Self-disciplined, and organized (one 8), this person is also an honest communicator who may be perceived as a bit too blunt (two 1s). However, unlike Example One, this person is emotionally sensitive, loyal, and tender-hearted, and will be deeply hurt by harsh comments or cruel gossip (negative arrow 3-5-7). Despite that, the person has practical skills and constructive talents that can lead to great good fortune and a lifetime of financial prosperity (positive line 8-1-6).

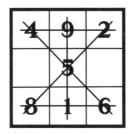

Example Three: The birth date is April 26th, 1958 or **4-2-6-1-9-5-8.**

This person is quiet (1), sensitive (2), orderly (4), emotionally stable (5), helpful (6), organized (8), and intelligent (9) — a combination that certainly foretells success. Additionally, this person has a high degree of intellect (positive line 4-9-2), a great deal of will power and self-assurance (positive line 9-5-1) and a strong drive to achieve wealth and prosperity (positive line 8-1-6). Driven by indomitable determination to advance at every opportunity and with persistence to stay the course (positive line 8-5-2), this person will nevertheless always humbly, and with sincere spiritual faith, cite Heaven's blessings and God's goodness as the reason for each personal success (positive line 4-5-6).

CHAPTER TWELVE
HOW THE NAME DISCLOSES THE FUTURE

YEAR-BY-YEAR FORECASTS FROM A NAME

We now proceed from character analysis to fortune telling.

Experience has demonstrated that each numerical vibration in a name endures, roughly speaking, one year, the time it takes the Earth to pass all the way around the Sun. The first letter in a birth name shows the character of the first year of the life, the second letter denotes the character of the second year, the third letter tells what is in store for the third year, and so on. Each letter is a vibration and each vibration is one year in length.

Having gone through the name one time, the cycle repeats, the duration of each repetition governed by the number of letters in the name. The longer the name, the longer the cycle, and the more opportunity for diverse experiences, as there are likely to be more letter-numbers in a longer name.

Take the following birth name, for example, and we will see how it tells the past and present, and discloses the future. Our subject is RANDOLPH JOHN WILLIAMS, age 30 years:

R	A	N	D	O	L	P	H		J	O	H	N		W	I	L	L	I	A	M	S
9	1	5	4	6	3	7	8		1	*6*	8	5		5	9	3	3	9	1	4	1

Age 1 2 3 4 5 6 7 8   9 10 11 12   13 14 15 16 17 18 19 20

*Age 21 22 23 24 25 26 27 28   29 **30** 31 32   33 34 35 36 37 38 39 40*

There are 20 letters in his name, so his pattern repeats every 20 years. Every letter-number appears in his name except the 2, so his experiences will be varied, although lacking in the particular yearly vibrations of the 2.

R is the first letter in his name, A is the second, N is the third, D is the fourth, and so on up to 30, his present age. This we see comes under the letter O or number **6**, so this, his 30th year, is in the 6th vibration.

His Destiny Number works out to an **8**, his Heart's Desire number is **5**, and he was born on April 8th, 1917, so his Life Path Number is a **3**.

His Personal Year runs from birthday to birthday. In this, his 30th Personal Year, he resonates to the number 6. His yearly outlook will assume the character of the humanitarian 6th vibration. He will find this year of his life not so strenuous as the previous year, which was indicated by a 1.

PROGRESSING THE NAME THROUGH THE YEARS

This is not the first time that RANDOLPH JOHN WILLIAMS has experienced a 6 vibration year. He previously felt the 6 when he was 5, 10, and 25 years old. In this 30th year of his existence, he will again cater to the peaceful, quiet, tranquil side of his life, for 6 is a number of peace, quiet, diplomacy, compassion, and repose.

His path this year will be less turbulent than the previous year. Humanity will give him a higher place in its regard and will look to him as a worthy individual. This, to him, will be a year of more mind rest, more tranquility, and fewer worries, as 6 is an optimistic, helpful number. It is, all told, a philanthropic, beneficial year, and coming, as it does, between the 1, (a rather pushing, active, forceful year), and the 8 (a thinking, critical, analytical business year), it should be of great benefit.

In this, his 30th year, more credence and reliance will be proffered him and the vibrations of blame and reproach and censure will not come his way as frequently as they have in certain other years of his life. This year will be most similar, generally speaking, to his 10th year, both coming under the same letter and the same numerical vibration.

His next year, when he assumes the age of 31, will be under the 8 vibration, it being the 31st age-letter in his name, and he will be at that time 31 years of age. This marks a change in his life, especially from his 30th year. His 31st year will be much more active and probably more materially remunerative, as 8 stands for worldly possessions and financial success. Furthermore, 8 is his Destiny Number, so he should make strides in his career, under an influence of power, enterprise, and expanding talents.

It is advisable that he achieve as much as possible in his 31st year, because the following two years, or his 32nd and 33rd, will be under the influence of the 5 and this, as we know, means change, indecision, travel, and lack of stability generally. However, 5 is also his Heart's Desire, and he is well adapted to changing scenes, and gains pleasure thereby.

His 34th year has indications, as told by the 9, that he will at that time take the broadest and most compassionate view of those around him.

It then comes about that the two years following this, which are his 35th and 36th years, will bring out his true expression, because his 35th and 36th years will be under the influence of the 3, an expressive number which also happens to be his lucky Birth Date or Life Path Number.

THE FUTURE IN A WOMAN'S BIRTH NAME

The mode of procedure in all cases is similar. First find the numbers in the name, each corresponding to a year in life; then look up the influences of the number and we have the general forecast for that year.

In the case of a married woman wishing to ascertain what vibration she is working under, she gives to each letter a year, as in the case of an unmarried woman or a man, but she uses her own given birth names, and not her married name. Thus, "Mrs. Henry Smith" is 25 and wishes to know the general trend of her next or 26th year. She takes her maiden name of JANE ELIZABETH BROWN and gives to each letter a year:

	J	A	N	E		E	L	I	Z	A	B	E	T	H		B	R	O	W	N
	1	1	5	5		5	3	9	**8**	1	2	5	2	8		2	9	6	5	5
Age	*1*	*2*	*3*	*4*		*5*	*6*	*7*	*8*	*9*	*10*	*11*	*12*	*13*		*14*	*15*	*16*	*17*	*18*
Age	*19*	*20*	*21*	*22*		*23*	*24*	*25*	***26***	*27*	*28*	*29*	*30*	*31*		*32*	*33*	*34*	*35*	*36*

She first puts the value of the letter of the name directly beneath, then proceeds to give each letter the value of one year, and we can see at a glance the general trend of her life, both of the past and present as well as the future. Her Destiny Number is **1**. Her Heart's Desire is **5.** We will say as a quick example that her birth date or lucky Life Path Number is **4.**

Her 26th year will be under the vibration of **8,** a year of advance in business and finances. She may well embark on a career or buy a home.

The **4** is her lucky Birth Date Number, but as there are no 4s in her name, she will never have any "lucky" years and may never be a bettor.

However, her Heart's Desire number is **5,** and having a stunning six examples of 5 in the eighteen letters of her name, she will have the good fortune to truly express herself in fully one-third of the years of her life.

PREDICTING A CHILD'S FUTURE

In a child's name, we must bear in mind its dependency upon its parents. As a result, the yearly number influence will not manifest as it does in those more advanced in years and more subject to their own judgement. Notice, for example, that our young Mrs. Smith's 26th year can hardly be said to compare to her 8th, although the vibration is the same number 8.

PARSING THE YEARLY NAME PREDICTION BY SEASON

To those desirous of looking deeper, seeking a more definite forecast than the yearly prediction, we may divide each year as does nature its seasons. From Winter to Summer, the Sun, as we see it, becomes more and more powerful in its influence, until the Summer climax is reached, after which it naturally declines and gradually sinks back to the dark of Winter.

In the same way, we may divide each letter in a name into seasons, and have the Spring, Summer, Autumn, and Winter of each letter. These will not be marked by the solstices and equinoxes, but rather from birthday to birthday, with each birth year divided into four quarters.

The first quarter-year, for three months after the birthday, is Spring: childhood, the plant pushing through the soil, the leaf-bud unfurling.

The second quarter-year of each letter represents Summer: youth, the flower blossoming, long days of sunshine, lightness, and gaiety.

The third quarter-year of the number is Autumn: the fruiting, the ripening, the reaping, and the falling away of its influence.

The fourth quarter-year of the number is Winter: age, the decline of its influence, the seed beneath a mantle of snow.

If a person is entering, say for instance, a number 2 year, the full influence is not immediately felt at the birthday, which is simply the Spring, childhood, or bud of the number 2, as gentleness and receptivity set in, and this lasts, roughly, for three months, or one fourth of a year.

In the second quarter, or Summer of this vibration, the influence naturally adjusts itself tighter around the individual. During this period the kindness of number 2 grows. This lasts until the end of the sixth month.

Then the Autumn, or reaping period, comes to its own. Here we find the person harvesting the benefits of several months of friendship and companionability, after which it gradually wanes in influence.

The last three months of the year, or the Winter of the 2, are marked by the decline of its essentially subjective and receptive influence. Its lesson having been learned, the person is ready for new experiences.

So, in entering onto a new yearly numerical vibration at the birthday, one does not feel its full force or power during the first quarter. The full strength is delayed in its influence, but it will develop in time. Again, on leaving the latter part of its run, the influence of the year's number is not greatly felt, due to its influence having gradually waned and declined.

CHAPTER THIRTEEN
DELIBERATELY VARYING THE SIGNATURE

THE INFLUENCE OF THE ATMOSPHERE

All events of this world, all happenings, circumstances, and undertakings have their separate, individual vibrations, and when we, as individuals, come in contact with these congregated vibrations, there is produced an amiable or adverse relationship.

"Atmospheres" are, as we know, mental oscillations or vibrations. They are originally produced by mental attitudes but eventually become so strong as to be individualized, and finally become so powerful as to be no longer affected by outside influences.

A church has a peculiar atmosphere or vibration which is said to be "characteristic of churches." Hence, we may say there is a "church vibration." This church vibration becomes impotent to individual attack, as is illustrated when we see some unbelieving and supposedly unbending and obstinate person, on entering the doors, lower his voice in intuitive acknowledgement of something more powerful than his skepticism.

Likewise, the dance hall, the stage, the theater, the business house, the professional rooms, the hospital, the banks, and countless other locations, all have their own characteristic and individualized vibrations.

We will receive more harmony, peace, and power from these vibrations or atmospheres, regardless of what they represent, by working in union with them, than we will by being antagonistic, even subconsciously so. While formerly we did not recognize it, we may now understand that we are subconsciously hostile when we carry a name that is not suitable to the atmosphere of the place which we enter. Man should be more elastic, not so unbending and unappreciative of the more subtle laws of life. He should learn to adjust, to cease forcing the vibrations where they are unsuitable and many times repugnant.

To assist in attaining this object of universal adjustment, one should have and use several names or signatures. That is, one's business signature should be agreeable and suitable to one's particular business, thus contributing toward and not detracting from its and one's ultimate success. If one becomes an orator, then, one should speak under a name that is harmonious and pleasing to the currents or vibrations of oratory.

THE IMPORTANCE OF SELF-SELECTED PSEUDONYMS

Let us co-operate with and adjust ourselves to that particular vibration under whose banner we wish to succeed. If it be on stage, then let us carry a theatrical name vibration, and not one of the hermit or close-mouthed recluse. If we desire musical success, let us endeavour to be amiable to the musical currents, and not antagonistic.

So it is with every conceivable career in life, in the arts, in politics, in the professions, and in business. If we are working in several branches of life, let us not strike one certain, unbending attitude and persistently carry it through all of the different branches from which we may be trying to wring success. We will attain much more by harmonizing and co-operating than through resistance and condemnation.

One good way to put one's self in harmonious union with any vibration is to sign the name with the letters whose numbers are in accord with the vibration and do not withdraw or detract from the general atmosphere of the endeavour. In other words, and to put it very tersely and concisely: Have a signature to meet every and all occasions.

1 is a signature to be used by explorers, heads of enterprises, directors, self-organizing planners, and motivators.

2 is a name for mothers, doctors, dentists, diplomats, arbitrators, and all of the less powerful and strenuous occupations.

3 is a successful vibration for singing, dancing, speaking, acting, entertaining, friendship, and joyful occupations.

4 is the number to adjust one's name to for a practical scientific career, country life, nature study, hunting, and to express stability.

5 is a number for action-oriented occupations, for travel, for the development of innovative ideas, and for the resourceful promoter.

6 is a positive name vibration for philanthropists, matrons, nurses, social workers, and humanitarians.

7 suits the religionists, inventors, stoics, meditators, mystics, and seekers after knowledge.

8 is a good business vibration, and is used by those seeking to express authority and gain recognition and financial independence.

9 is a signature of the broad-minded universalist; it also suits the minister, the artist, and the sincere altruist.

CAN A STRONG SURNAME "FIX" DISCORDANT NAMES?

In designing a successful name for the stage or to use as a nom de plume, it is important to keep the several single names harmonious, and to also choose for a powerful whole. The surname is generally the solid foundation upon which the several single names are chosen, but after choosing them, it is also a good idea to consider the Destiny Number, that is, the reduction from the sum total of all the names assembled.

Do not expect the surname to "fix" a series of discordantly numbered names merely because it allows for an appropriate Destiny Number.

A weak or inapprorpiate Destiny Number obtained by adding together discordant names will not manifest the same qualities as a strong Destiny Number which is composed only of harmonious single names, but a strong and appropriate Destiny Number composed of discordant single names is like a family divided against itself. While it may eventually be successful, yet the process of attainment is difficult and disagreeable.

Now, just as a suitable Destiny Number derived from discordant single names is not an entirely happy combination, neither is it wise to choose a combination of strong and appropriately numbered single 0names if their union makes for a weak and inappropriate Destiny Number. Many people are "near geniuses." Continually on the brink of great things, they almost attain to fame and opulence in their chosen line, yet, despite their apparent worthiness, there is always a "something" that intervenes to keep the object, success, forever out of their eager grasp. It is "Oh, so near!" and yet, always "so far."

An individual of the "near genius" class of persons may appear to have a strong surname and a personally appropriate Destiny Number, but, on closer analysis, the fly in the ointment is usually found in a first or middle name with a weak or inappropriate vibration and which is just powerful enough to keep the other names from exerting their best influence.

To sum up, the separate single names of the professional name ought to make for harmony. These single names should agree with the surname, with the Destiny Number, and with each other. If the name-numbers can also relate harmoniously to the Heart's Desire Number or vowel sum, the Persona Number or consonant sum, and to the Life Path or Birth Date Number, then, like a train whose gears are all in synchrony, we have a name that tells the world who we are and will get us where we want to go.

HARMONIOUS NUMBERS

1 agrees, or has many things in common with 4, 8.
2 agrees, or has many things in common with 7, 9.
3 agrees, or has many things in common with 5, 6, 9.
4 agrees, or has many things in common with 1, 8.
5 agrees, or has many things in common with 3.
6 agrees, or has many things in common with 3, 7, 9.
7 agrees, or has many things in common with 2, 6.
8 agrees, or has many things in common with 1, 4.
9 agrees, or has many things in common with 2, 3, 6.

DISCORDANT NUMBERS

1 is not in harmony with names vibrating to 7.
2 is not in harmony with names vibrating to 5.
3 is not in harmony with names vibrating to 4, 7.
4 is not in harmony with names vibrating to 3, 5.
5 is not in harmony with names vibrating to 2, 7, 8.
6 is satisfied with any number and feels no disharmony.
7 is not in harmony with names vibrating to 3, 5, 9.
8 is not in harmony with names vibrating to 5.
9 is not always happy with names vibrating to 7.

Number 1 and Number 2 have a strange mutual influence. They are opposite in their natural tendencies, yet when combined as first and middle names, they are beneficial to a full name. This is accountable principally to the soothing, pacifying, modifying influence of the 2. A typical 1's characteristics for briskness and mastery is quieted by the gentle subtlety and quiet persuasive powers of the 2. Hence the name MAE which vibrates 1 (M is 4, A is 1, E is 5; 4 plus 1 plus 5 = 10: and 1 plus 0 = 1) would be benefitted and softened by joining with the name IVY, which vibrates 2 (I is 9, V is 4, Y is 7: 9 plus 4 plus 7 = 20; and 2 plus 0 = 2). There is a further benefit in that IVY MAE is a "pretty" name.

Number 6 has no "enemies" at all; it ranges from congenial to neutral.

Number 9 is not antagonistic to any number, but it obtains better opportunity for expression with a congenial number such as 2, 3, or 6.

COMPARE THE LIFE PATH TO THE DESTINY NUMBER

Before deciding to change the presented name, and its numbers with it, compare the Life Path Number and the Destiny Number for harmony or discord. The Life Path tells what we have brought with us; what we will do is told by the Destiny Number. The Life Path number provides a benchmark from which to gauge the outcome in the Destiny Number.

Life Path and Destiny Number Discordant: We often find people who were born with the ability to be great in a particular field, but all this power is going to waste while they give their time to other things, either willingly or because they are required to do so by existing circumstances or external conditions. Among such people it is very likely that we will find those whose Life Path and Destiny Number are at odds or variance.

For example, take a life whose Destiny Number is 8, which means it must rule and control in business. If the birth number is a 2, the lesson is apt to be a difficult one, for number 2 is gentle, quiet, and retiring, so the individual learning the lesson of vibration 8 would find that he often lacked the courage, command, and control necessary to master the financial world.

If the Life Path is receptive and the Destiny Number active, the individual may fail to achieve great success. If the Life Path is strong and the Destiny Number passive, the power that is behind the life will help the individual get over the difficult places that appear on the path.

Life Path and Destiny Number Harmonious: When the Life Path and the Destiny Number are in accord, the individual naturally "grows into" a suitable and fortuitous occupation with easy adjustment.

For instance, if the Life Path is 1 and the Destiny Number is 8, the person is born strong, determined, and unafraid, easily overcoming and surmounting all difficulties, and filled with do-and-dare spirit, so nothing would stand in his way as he entered the business world.

If both the Life Path and the Destiny Number are active, we have a positive character. If they are both receptive, the character is receptive.

Life Path and Destiny Number Identical: When the Life Path and the Destiny Number are identical, the person follows the line of work he or she was born to do, often from a precociously early age.

RECTIFYING YOUR NAME

The first, middle, and last name of an individual may agree among themselves and be harmonious, or they may disagree among themselves and be antagonistic one to the other, and, as a result, cause inharmony and subconscious turmoil.

A harmonious name is generally recognized, at least subconsciously, as "easy on the ears" or "pretty" or having a "dignified" quality.

Inharmonious names, however, are often difficult to understand as such. They produce a sense of turmoil and unease which may be recognized as existing, but which, until one applies Numerology to the question, may be difficult or impossible to identify. The trouble is rarely with the name as a whole; it is generally with the component names.

Let us consider the Vernons. They wish to name their baby boy, and, for reasons barely considered, they select the old family names George and Walter as his first and middle names. Unfortunately, GEORGE is the emotional opposite to WALTER:

G E O R G E	W A L T E R	V E R N O N
7 5 6 9 7 5	5 1 3 2 5 9	4 5 9 5 6 5
39	25	34
3	**7**	**7**

WALTER is a number 7, known for meditative quiet, introspection, and reclusive poise, while the 3 of GEORGE is expressive, entertaining, and outgoing. Neither is "bad" or "wrong," but opposition is personified in these names. One is continually pulling against the other, the natural result being that the bearer of such a name carries with him a sense of disharmony. Because his surname, VERNON, is also a 7, he is certain to feel that the source of this perpetual discord is his first name, GEORGE. It is very likely that he will drop his first name and be known thenceforward as WALTER VERNON, because he "never did like the name George anyhow."

If your parents did not consider Numerology when naming you, you may have a set of names that disagree with one another, and these names may unconsciously add a link to that chain of inharmony that exists in all lives and which everyone is perpetually endeavouring to eradicate. You can change this, though. The name you present to the public is yours to choose.

ELIMINATING DISCORDANT NAMES

Usually, some of the single names of the whole name are harmonious with other single names in the complete name, while again, a complete name may contain single names which are out of harmony with another, and so make for discord in the entire name.

Elimination is one remedy for this name discordance. As an instance, take a complete name composed of three single names, only two of which agree, and for effective redress cease to use the odd or disagreeing name. This is a very forceful remedy as it cuts off the discordant current at its source or fountainhead.

```
J  A  M  E  S      H  E  N  R  Y      J  U  S  T  I  C  E
1  1  4  5  1      8  5  5  9  7      1  3  1  2  9  3  5
      12                  34                    24
       3                   7                     6
```

In this name, disharmony exists between JAMES (3), and HENRY (7). One is oil and the other water, and as a result, there is no mixing or blending. If the bearer of this name is to make what we call a "success," it will be so in spite of circumstances, situation, or condition.

To harmonize the above name, the best way is to cease signing the middle name HENRY, using only the names JAMES and JUSTICE. The first name JAMES being a 3 and the surname JUSTICE being a 6, these names are in harmonious relationship. Together they produce a Destiny Number of 9, which harmonizes with both names.

Similarly, our unfortunate GEORGE (3) WALTER (7) VERNON (7) would do well to drop the first name GEORGE and go forth as WALTER (7) VERNON (7), as the twin 7s are harmonious. However, the Destiny Number is then 5 (7 plus 7 = 14; and 1 plus 4 = 5), and 5 is not notably harmonious to 7. He will do the best he can, by shedding the unwanted GEORGE, but his parents, knowing that VERNON (7) was a given, would have done better to have named him WALTER (7) ANDREW (2) VERNON (7) for a Destiny Number of 7 (7 plus 2 plus 7 = 16; and 1 plus 6 = 7). Had that been the case, the gentle 2 of ANDREW in the middle would have harmonized the flanking 7s, and produced the surprise Destiny Number of 7 that agrees with both WALTER and VERNON.

HOW CHANGING THE SPELLING CHANGES ONE'S LIFE

Our continual aim should always be to use names which are suitable or acceptable one to the other. Having several names, you will do best to use only those that co-operate and work together in unison. Also endeavour, as far as possible, to strengthen your potentialities and inherent powers by keeping the single names in unison with the Destiny Number.

One of the most subtle ways to bring discordant names into harmony is to slightly change the spelling of one name, or use it in nickname form, or only use it as an initial. This example should give you some ideas:

ANTHONY DONALD NAPOLITANO
TONY D. NAPOLITANO
"TONY D"

ANTHONY (7) DONALD (5) NAPOLITANO (9), with a Destiny Number of 3, is not harmonious. The 7 of ANTHONY is inharmonious to the 5 of DONALD, and to the 9 of NAPOLITANO, and also to the Destiny Number of 3.

TONY (2) D. (4) NAPOLITANO (9), with a Destiny Number of 6, is different. It is an easy-going and fairly harmonious name because the 2 of TONY harmonizes with the 9 of NAPOLITANO, while the Destiny Number of 6 is generally harmonious with all numbers.

If he goes by the nickname TONY D., the 2 and the 4 sum to 6, his Destiny Number. While not his "legal" name, this name makes him happy.

QUICK TRICK: CASTING OUT NINES

Summing the names ANTHONY (7) DONALD (5) NAPOLITANO (9) to get the Destiny Number 3 and TONY (2) D. (4) NAPOLITANO (9) to get the Destiny Number 6 brings up a quick trick that most Numerologists, and just about all mathematicians know — casting out nines.

Any time you have a string of numbers to add and you want to work so quickly that producing a complete draw-down is not important, just eliminate every 9 you get to. 7 plus 5 plus 9 = 21 and 1 plus 2 = **3**. But cast out the 9 and you'll see: 7 plus 5 = 12 and 1 plus 2 = **3**, just the same.

Try it on 2 plus 4 plus 9 versus 2 plus 4. See? That's casting out nines!

CHAPTER FOURTEEN
NAMES SUITABLE FOR A BUSINESS

SELECTING A BUSINESS NAME

Just like people, business enterprises have names — and those names have numbers. When selecting a business name, you are, consciously or unconsciously, encoding within it a numerical signature.

Astrologers fix the horoscope of a business from the day of its founding. You can work out a Life Path Number or Lo Shu Square for that date, but also check the full name or Destiny Number of the business, as used on articles of incorporation, store signage, or digital media. Pages 28, 30, and 60 have Destiny Number details. These samples will help you get the idea:

An art gallery, dance studio, or theater vibrates well to the Number 3:

UPTOWN   DANCE   CLUB
3 7 2 6 5 5   4 1 5 3 5   3 3 3 2
= 57; 5 plus 7 = 12; 1 plus 2 = **3.**

For free-lance and contract labour in the trades, choose the Number 4:

BILL'S   MOBILE   WELDING
2 9 3 3 1   3 6 2 9 3 5   5 5 3 4 9 5 7
= 85; 8 plus 5 = 13; 1 plus 3 = **4.**

If your business deals with financial investments, go with Number 8:

ROSEDALE   PROPERTY   MANAGEMENT
9 6 1 5 4 1 3 5   7 9 6 7 5 9 2 7   4 1 5 1 7 5 4 5 5 2
= 125; 1 plus 2 plus 5 = **8.**

To teach without profit, for the benefit of all, select Master Number 11:

LUCKY   MOJO   CURIO   CO.
3 3 3 2 7   4 6 1 6   3 3 9 9 6   3 6
= 74; 7 plus 4 = **11.**

NAMES SUITABLE FOR AN AUTHOR

At this point, i, catherine yronwode, wish to step out from behind the curtain of authorial collaboration with the dead. In editing the previous material on pseudonyms and rectifications, i was struck by something that my mysterious co-author, Dr. Roy Page Walton, had to say on the subject:

"I know an adjustable individual who is fundamentally a professional man. He dabbles in business and, on occasion, writes and lectures. For each different vocation he has a different name, never using his business signature at the head of his articles, nor signing his professional name on his books. His several signatures are used for his several undertakings.

"He varies the sound of his name, adding or dropping one name of his several, or using an initial in place of a name — all done to keep his name and the thing he is doing harmonious to one another. A simple change of spelling alters the name in value. History tells us of many instances of how changes of name affected individual lives and circumstances."

ROY PAGE WALTON is 22-2-22 or 4-2-4. It reduces to 10, and then to 1. This is a nicely balanced name, the symmetry of the whole reinforced by the symmetrical vowels, O A E A O (6-1-5-1-6, reducing to 4).

On the other hand, let us examine the pseudonym of the plagiarist, LEWIS DE CLAREMONT. Although this is supposedly the name of a man who wrote a book on Numerology, it violates the very principles on which the book is founded, for his first and last names are inharmonious when reduced: LEWIS = 5 and DE CLAREMONT = 2. The sum is 7.

One year later, the book was republished under the revised pseudonym GODFREY SPENCER, which perfectly upholds the tenets of Numerology. Both names have a letter-count of 7, both GODFREY and SPENCER reduce to 8, a state of harmonious financial unity, and 8 plus 8 is 16 = 7.

As revealed on page 80, my birth name is CATHERINE (47 = 11) and my birth date is May 12th, 1947 (47 = 11). However, my surname YRONWODE, with its unusual spelling and its sum of 47 = 11, is one that my ex-partner Peter and i worked out in 1969 to suit our own personal numerological goals. Of course, 4711 Cologne is my favourite brand of perfume — and, as noted on page 67, the spiritual supply house i founded is the LUCKY MOJO CURIO CO., which has a sum of 74 = 11.

CHAPTER FIFTEEN
NAMES SUITABLE FOR A MARRIAGE

Despite a prolific abundance of opinions and advice written on this subject, individuals contemplating entering into what the newspapers call "marital bliss" generally do so regardless of whether they are, according to some "sage's" system, in "perfect accord" or "perfect soul unison." Nevertheless, such a system of evaluation does exist in Numerology, as it does in Astrology, and it can easily be explained.

The law of happy unions in Numerology is based upon the Law of Similarities. In other words, the numerical analysis of the individuals must be similar, if happiness is to be the result,

Now, it is an old idea that harmonious union is based upon the so-called Law of Opposites, or the saying that "opposites attract." Many people have taken to themselves their direct opposite for a mate — opposite in word, thought, action, and deed. Many marry opposites because they are attracted by certain qualities in the other which they themselves do not possess.

Under the Law of Opposites, for example, we often see a powerful, rugged, muscular man become enchanted by a physically frail, dainty woman. Likewise, the delicate creature is attracted to his magnetism, force, and majestic physique, qualities she surely lacks.

She relies on his energy, strength, and power, and feels a safety and comfort hitherto foreign to her. He looks to her to satisfy his creature comforts, including food and drink when and how he likes it. He does not understand her interest in spirituality, artistry, and music. She grows tired of cooking for him. He wearies of what he calls her "silly emotions," her love of the beauties in Nature, her talk of the "God in the Woods."

To him, her interests are intangible and meaningless, while to her, his world of beefsteak and physical feats has become too tangible, so, as a natural result, the inevitable happens, and the marriage is a failure.

The physical man then takes a great cook to be his wife and she prepares for him all the exotic foods of all the world, with wine and beers to match. The frail woman takes a poet to be her husband and at dusk they sit on the porch together and marvel at the fireflies. And all is well.

In choosing marriageable names, let us therefore bear in mind the Law of Similarities. The more numerical harmonies, and the fewer numerical discords, the better is the opportunity for a continued amiable union.

WILL THIS MARRIAGE BE SUCCESSFUL?

JAMES RALPH HOMES and ANNIE LAURA PEAKE are in love and they wish to marry. Let us see how good a choice they have made:

COMPARE THE TOTAL NUMBER OF LETTERS

The number of letters in JAMES RALPH HOMES is 15 and ANNIE LAURA PEAKE also has 15 letters. The total number of letters need not be an exact match for harmony, but it is well to have them as near as possible.

COMPARE THE FREQUENCY OF THE NUMBERS

The numerals in their names and the number of times they occur bear observation. *Italic* numbers placed directly below the name indicate the range from 1 through 9. **Bold** numbers below those indicate the frequency of their occurrence in the name; a dash shows numbers which are missing.

J A M E S   R A L P H   H O M E S
1 1 4 5 1   9 1 3 7 8   8 6 4 5 1

Numerals *1 2 3 4 5 6 7 8 9*
Frequency **5 (-) 1 2 2 1 1 2 1**

The number 2 is missing in his name. He is very strong on the number 1, with 5 occurrences. None of his other numbers rise above 2. Let us now treat the woman's name in the same manner.

A N N I E   L A U R A   P E A K E
1 5 5 9 5   3 1 3 9 1   7 5 1 2 5

Numerals *1 2 3 4 5 6 7 8 9*
Frequency **4 1 2 (-) 5 (-) 1 (-) 2**

The numbers missing in her name are the 4, the 6, and the 8. Her strongest number is the 5, which occurs 5 times, followed by the modestly strong number 1, which occurs 4 times.

COMPARE THE HARMONIES TO THE DISCORDS

Now we can compare these two names under the Law of Similarities. Each letter in his name that is also in her name contributes toward their soul union, and each letter in either name not contained in the other name, or occurring in unlike frequency, acts as a subconscious barrier to blissful marriage. Individual numbers occur several times in each name and while there can, of course, be no arbitrary rule, it is fairly safe to say that:

- The harmonious numbers are those appearing a like number of times in the names of both parties, where one name possesses it only one time more, or one time less, than does the other name.
- When one name has a complete absence of a number that does occur in the other name, even if only once, that is not harmonious, for although the difference in frequency is but one, the complete lack of a shared number leaves that unmatched number nothing upon which to build in the way of similarity.
- When both names contain a number, but one name has it in great excess of the other, we cannot call it a harmonious vibration. For instance, one name has, let us say, six 3s, and the other name contains only three 3s; we cannot call it harmony. This will be explained more fully after we analyze the names now under consideration.

	JAMES RALPH HOMES	ANNIE LAURA PEAKE	Result
Number of Letters	Fifteen	Fifteen	Harmony
The number 1	Five Times	Four Times	Harmony
The number 2	Absent	Once	Discord
The number 3	Once	Twice	Harmony
The number 4	Twice	Absent	Discord
The number 5	Twice	Five Times	Discord
The number 6	Once	Absent	Discord
The number 7	Once	Once	Harmony
The number 8	Twice	Absent	Discord
The number 9	Once	Twice	Harmony

A FIFTY-FIFTY CHANCE

Comparing the numbers in their names that are in harmony, due to their similar frequency of occurrence, with the numbers in which they are discordant or out of harmony, due to disparate frequency, we cannot call the names JAMES RALPH HOMES and ANNIE LAURA PEAKE suitable for harmonious marital co-operation.

- Considering the number of letters, both have 15. This is harmonious.
- Under the number 1, they are harmonious, because they both have this vibration occurring numerous times in their names.
- They are inharmonious on the number 2, because, while she only possesses it once, he owns it not at all.
- On the 3, the two names are harmonious, because they both include it in near-like frequency.
- On the 4, they are inharmonious, as he has it twice, and she not at all.
- On the 5, they are inharmonious, because while they both possess this number, she does so too often to be harmonious with him, she having the 5 occur five times to his twice.
- On the 6, they are inharmonious, as while he only possesses one 6 in his name, she possesses none.
- On the 7, they are harmonious, both possessing one 7.
- On the 8, they are inharmonious, as he has it twice and she not at all.
- On the 9, they are harmonious, she with two 9s to his one.

Therefore, of the nine numerals, indicating nine different points of understanding on which to be harmonious, they are only so four times. Only four out of nine, fewer than half. The inharmony outweighs the harmony, as the former has five out of a possible nine.

Even with the total number of letters being in harmony, as both are 15, this still amounts to only five out of ten chances for marital concord, a 50-50 proposition that they will find true wedded bliss.

BUT — before we write this couple off completely, let us speculate that instead of merely living together, they wed one another and she, being a traditionalist, chooses to accept his surname as her own.

What are the chances for a harmonious and long-lasting marriage between JAMES RALPH HOMES and ANNIE LAURA HOMES?

JAMES RALPH HOMES AND ANNIE LAURA HOMES

Amazingly, when she takes his surname, she gains the missing 4, 6, and 8 that kept them apart. She loses a 2, and now they match on 2, as both have none. She loses a 7, while he still has his. Her 5s come down to four, which still fails to balance with his two 5s. but, miraculously, they still both have the same total number of letters, 15. This gives us a very different picture:

J A M E S   R A L P H   H O M E S
1 1 4 5 1   9 1 3 7 8   8 6 4 5 1

Numerals	1	2	3	4	5	6	7	8	9
Frequency	5	(-)	1	2	2	1	1	2	1

A N N I E   L A U R A   H O M E S
1 5 5 9 5   3 1 3 9 1   8 6 4 5 1

Numerals	1	2	3	4	5	6	7	8	9
Frequency	4	(-)	2	1	4	1	(-)	1	2

- On the number of letters, both have 15, which is harmonious.
- On the 1 they are harmonious, at five and four in frequency.
- On the 2 they are harmonious, as both have none.
- On the 3 they are harmonious, with near-like frequency.
- On the 4 they are harmonious, as he has it twice, and she owns it once.
- On the 5 they are discordant, because she has four 5s to his two.
- On the 6 they are harmonious, as they each possesses one 6.
- On the 7 they are discordant, as he has one 7 and she has none.
- On the 8 they are harmonious, as he has it twice and she has it once.
- On the 9 they are harmonious, with her two to his one.

If she changes her surname to his, they now have EIGHT points of harmony out of a possible ten points, and a very good chance of wedded union. Note well that it is SHE who will make most of the adjustments. This is not to say that a woman must always take a man's surname to enjoy a happy marriage, or that she must adopt his ways for the good of the relationship, but for this couple, such seems to be the case.

CHAPTER SIXTEEN
CHOOSING THE BEST NAME FOR A CHILD

THE SELECTION SHOULD BE A CONSCIOUS ONE

Naming a child represents, as parents will recall, a period of deep reflection, studied contemplation, and occasional all-round indecision. Choosing the name is of more vital importance than irresolute parents realize. They worry over their selection, and were you to ask them why they worry, they probably could not give a rational answer, but they feel subconsciously the deep importance attached to the naming ceremony.

Names were formerly, and are even today, chosen by the uninitiated in a promiscuous fashion. They close their eyes and select blindly, only hoping that their choice turns out suitably for the worthy offspring. Their moment of wavering choice, worry, and vagueness is often the result of ignorance or an attempt to please other family members, while remaining uncertain of how to please the child-to-be.

However, the time is not far distant when we will proceed to the choosing of a child's name as we proceed to the solving of any problem, not from guesswork or from an unlearned standpoint, but rather from intellectual comprehension, augmented by true spiritual insight.

No longer, then, will we name the first-born son Willie because his financially successful uncle goes by the name of William. Neither will we name a child after his father, simply because the father thinks it such a manly name and so perfectly suited for his manly little infant. Instead, we will combine harmony in sound with numerological principles to convey a traditional name of value or to create a new name of great promise.

THE SURNAME IS HEREDITARY

For hundreds of years the "father-right" of granting the surname to a child has allowed hereditary names to remain undeviating in construction and relatively constant in their letters. However, in some families it is the practice to simplify the spelling of ancient or foreign-sounding names. Always remember, though, that when the spelling changes, even by one letter, the numerical vibration of the name changes as well.

HARMONIZING THE GIVEN NAME AND SURNAME

The first or personal name should be our working key for a successful choice of names. We have only to bear the following rules in mind:

- Old family given names, such as Thomas, William, John, or Isaac, remain mostly unchangeable, but you should select the one most in rapport with the surname. That is, if the last name vibrates to 7, do not choose a first name vibrating to 3.
- In selecting or creating a new or novel given name, the same principle should apply. Numerically, it should harmonize with the surname.
- If a nickname is selected, it should harmonize with the given name.
- If possible, the given name, surname, and nickname, should all vibrate to numbers that have inherent sympathy for one another.
- The sum total of letters in the given name should be in harmony with the sum total in the last name. For instance, if the last name is Smith, a word of 5 letters, do not choose a name like Rolland which has 7 letters, as 5 and 7 do not harmonize, and there is no advantage to be gained by tying or hinging these unfriendly vibrations even in this small way. Rather, choose a name containing 3 letters, because 3 and 5 are amiable, or 5 letters, because the 5 and the 5 express unity.

WHICH PARENT WILL THE CHILD FAVOUR?

When choosing the infant's name, the Law of Inheritance must also be taken into careful consideration. The several natural predominating qualities of the family should be analyzed and reviewed. An old saying has it that a professional or mechanical man is "born and not made," and the unbiased observer will appreciate that this is a great part of the truth. The general outcome of the artistic parent is the artistic child, and the progeny of the mechanical parent usually has a mechanical turn.

When the parents come under the Law of Opposites, that is, one being scientific and the other, for instance, artistic, and doubt exists as to which way the child will turn, there are two popular, if not infallible rules: We may assume the child will take on the characteristics of the stronger parent; or we may assume that the male child will "take after" his father, in the main, and the female child will "take after" the mother.

WHEN THERE IS A "BENT" IN THE FAMILY

When we are satisfied that the child has a "bent" towards mechanics, because from his great-grandfather to the present, all of the men of the family have been engineers, then give him a mechanical name, that is any name relating to the numbers 4 or 8, the leaders in this department.

When the family is artistic, then they are safe in bestowing on the child an artistic name vibrating to 3, 6 or 9. If one name vibrates to 6, let the other contain three, six, or nine letters and if it vibrates to 9, let it contain three, six, or nine letters. If possible let all the names vibrate to 3, 6, or 9.

When the child is destined for leading large organizations, inventing, and planning, names vibrating to 1 will contribute to his or her success.

When oratory, acting, or painting are anticipated, a name vibrating to 3 is acceptable; 9 is also good, as is 6 in a lesser degree.

- **1:** Entrepreneurs, heads of corporations, explorers, innovators, leaders, and planners vibrate well to names that reduce to a 1.
- **2:** For diplomacy, ministry, private secretaryship, arbitration, and certain branches of medicine and dentistry, a 2 name is best.
- **3:** Acting, singing, dancing, entertaining from the stage, wit, and inspirational verbal facility co-operate agreeably with a 3 name.
- **4:** Foremen, those who combine mental and physical traits, practical scientists, and those who work outdoors will do well with a 4 name.
- **5:** Occupations that call for adaptability, fascination, versatility, and occupations that involve travel do well with the 5 name.
- **6:** Humanitarians, philanthropists, artistic workers, and community organizers work best with a 6 name.
- **7:** The mystic, recluse, abstract thinker, philosopher, and solitary inventor further their aim with a 7 name.
- **8:** For technicians, statistical analysts, and those pursuing financial business success it is wise to select the 8 name.
- **9:** The 9 vibration is virtuous and enduring, making it beneficial for musicians, actors, orators, and ministers.

But note well — you may wish to hold back on the final name choice until the child is born, so that the Birth Date or Life Path Number can be added to the Destiny Number, to create a harmonious Vocational Number!

CHAPTER SEVENTEEN
LUCKY DREAM BOOKS FOR PLAYING POLICY, THE NUMBERS, AND LOTTERIES

POLICY KINGS AND QUEENS

Today most people are familiar with the various state lotteries, not knowing that the popular Pick-Three and Mega-Ball type games derive from an old illegal lottery system known as Policy or The Numbers.

Policy was an illegal lottery first introduced in Chicago in 1885 by an African-American operator nicknamed Policy Sam. It soon spread around the country and, despite anti-policy laws, which started appearing on the books as early as 1901, it flourished everywhere in America until legal state lotteries supplanted it.

Eventually the use of the term "policy" for this type of game came to imply an African-American clientele, for among Italian-Americans a similar illegal lottery was called "the Numbers," while Cuban-Americans in New York referred to their numbered ball lottery as "Bolita."

Policy bets were placed on groups of numbers from 1 through 78 (coincidentally the number of cards in a tarot deck). Borrowing from horse-racing terminology, a two-number betting combination was called a "saddle," a three-number combination a "gig," and a four-number combination a "horse." Gigs were the most popular play, but bets could be made in combinations of up to 25 numbers. Some gigs were so well-known that they had their own names, such as "the washerwoman's gig" (4-11-44) and "the dirty gig" (3-6-9). In the 19th century, a wager could be as low as one cent per number or three cents per gig; by the 1930s most operators set a three-cent or nickel lower limit on bets. The payout was usually ten-to-one, but higher payouts were made for groups of numbers.

In the early years, winning policy bets were selected several times a day, when those who ran the game spun a large wheel and "the numbers fell." The "companies" that operated policy wheels gave themselves (and thereby their wheels) colourful names, such as "The Interstate," "The East & West," "The Red Devil," "The Dead Row," and "The Streamliner."

Those who operated policy companies were called "Bankers," and the most successful were "Kings" or "Queens." Many became millionaires.

PLAYING THE NUMBERS

In New York City in the 1920s, policy operators tampered with their wheels so often that an "honest" version of the game was established in which bets were taken on the last three numbers of the daily Federal Reserve Clearing House Report. "Clearing-House" was immune to charges of corruption, and offered the further advantage that the bettor did not need to contact a runner to learn if he or she had won, because the numbers were printed in the daily newspapers. Another New York game, the "Mutuel Number," was calculated from payouts at horse tracks. In the South, "The Cotton Exchange" derived its winning numbers from the daily spot prices for cotton on the Chicago Board of Trade.

USING DREAM BOOKS TO CATCH LUCKY NUMBERS

Mystical dream books supply psychological interpretations of dreams, but lucky dream books like *Aunt Sally's Policy Players, Rajah Rabo's Pick 'Em, Kansas City Kitty, Three Wisemen,* and *The H.P.,* provide numbers you can bet on. These books link dream images ("a cook" or "a locomotive") to digits (5-14-50 or 65-41-55), and some also include divinations ("You will receive a letter" or "Beware a strange man"). Many are so popular that they have remained in print for more than 100 years — but if you think that's old, consider *Zhōu Gōng Jiě Mèng (The Interpretation of Dreams by the Duke of Zhou),* a Chinese text that gives four-digit betting numbers for dreams (e.g. "Uncle: 0495 or 2495" and "Tortoise: 0694 or 2694"). It is attributed to Zhōu Gōng, an author who lived more than 3,000 years ago!

In a lottery dream book, the dreams are listed in alphabetical order, with numbers beside them, for the convenience of bettors. Not all dream books agree on which numbers are linked to which dreams, but these are typical:

- **Butter:** Some good fortune, but mixed with sadness. — 4, 7, 13.
- **Fan:** Your mistress will be inconstant. — 5, 23, 31.
- **Judge:** You will overcome an enemy. — 28, 50, 70.
- **Ladder:** If going up, wealth; if coming down, poverty. — 11, 31, 43.

Read more about dream books and how to use them in gambling here: **LuckyMojo.com/auntsallys.html by Catherine Yronwode**

CHAPTER EIGHTEEN
FOLLOW-UPS AND RUN-DOWNS

THE LEGACY OF POLICY AND THE NUMBERS

Three-digit lotteries often feature Straight Play, in which the numbers drawn must match your three numbers in exact order, and Box Play, in which they can match your numbers in any order. This type of bet, in which Straight pays out higher than Box, derives from the old game of Policy, as seen in the 1920s *Kansas City Kitty Dream Book,* where a preacher standing in the pulpit tells his parishioners, "If you must play 'em, Box 'em!"

FOLLOW-UPS BY LAST DRAWN NUMBER

Follow-Ups are "relative" numbers believed likely to follow a winning number. You can use your birth date number to generate Follow-Ups. If the Last Drawn Number was **492** and your birth date is July 17, 1974 (7-1-7-1-9-7-4 = **36**), you add 492 plus 36 = **528** and you play 528 Straight and Boxed. Next day, add 36 again (528 plus 36 = **564**) and play it Straight and Boxed. Do this for seven days before choosing a new Last Drawn Number.

FOLLOW-UPS BY NUMERICAL PERMUTATION

To run permutations as Follow-Ups, play your original three-digit number Straight and Boxed, and if it does not win, put it through daily "changes." For example, if your number is **492**, play it Straight and Boxed, then on the next day, play **429** Straight and Boxed, on the third day play **924** Straight and Boxed, and on through **942, 249,** and **294** the same way. This gives five days of numbers as Follow-Ups to the original number.

FOLLOW-UPS BY THE BOOK

There are dozens of well-known systems for disclosing Follow-Ups, and many of them can be found in books like *Prof. Hitt's Rundowns & Workouts, Billy Bing's Work-Out Book,* and *Billy Bing's Red Book of Relative Numbers: Follow-Ups.* See more about Follow-Ups here:
LuckyMojo.com/auntsallys.html by Catherine Yronwode

AN OLD-TIME WORK-OUT WITH MAJORS AND MINORS

Run-Downs, Draw-Downs, and Work-Outs are systems that disclose derivaative betting numbers. This is Mrs. Hare's and Mr. Murray's old-fashioned Work-Out method. Digits are added by pairs. Three- or four-digit numbers are not allowed. Addition proceeds from left to right, and "odd" numbers are "carried" down until they find a "partner." Birth dates are included with the name. If a Master Number like 11 is final, it does not reduce. "Majors" are numbers to keep in play. "Minors" are add-ons.

```
C - A - T - H - E - R - I - N - E
3 - 1 - 2 - 8 - 5 - 9 - 9 - 5 - 5
  - 4 - - 10 - - 14 - - 14 - 5 -
  - - 14 - - - - - - - 28 - - 5 - -
  - - - - - 42 - - - - - - - 5 - - - -
  - - - - - - - - 47 - - - - - - - - -
  - - - - - - - - 11 - - - - - - - - -


Y - R - O - N - W - O - D - E
7 - 9 - 6 - 5 - 5 - 6 - 4 - 5
  - 16 - - 11 - - 11 - - 9 -
  - - - 27 - - - - - - - 20 - - -
  - - - - - - - 47 - - - - - - -
  - - - - - - - 11 - - - - - - -


        5 - 12 - 19 - 47
        - 17 - - 19 - 11 -
        - - 36 - - 11 - -
        - - - - 47 - - - -
        - - - - 11 - - - -
```

In this example, **47** and **11** are lucky Majors or semi-final and final sums, the best to bet. **47** (4 plus 7) self-sums to **11** three times. Numbers **14** and **5** are moderately lucky Minors or high-freqency interior sums. **14** (1 plus 4) self-sums to **5** three times, and **5** appears ten times, but never as a Major.

The lucky days to bet, according to this personal run-down, are the 5th, 11th, and 14th days of the 5th and 11th months (May and November).

CHAPTER NINETEEN
THE LUCKY NUMBER MASTER CODE
OF LEWIS DE CLAREMONT

As many lottery players know, the chief problem with pre-written dream books is that your dream may not be included in the list. Such books provide no way to work out a dream, a name, or an omen that they do not enumerate. This is where having access to a Master Code proves useful. A personal Master Code will allow you to generate your own three-digit numbers for any dreams, names, omens, or words you desire.

Master Codes may be created by noting previous wins or by a system as simple as rolling three dice and reducing numbers higher than nine.

DE CLAREMONT'S MASTER CODE OF LUCKY NUMBERS

Beside each code number is a series of three-digit numbers, in which the first is emphasized as the key, core, or Major three-digit combination. the highest vibration and the most important number for that Code Number. The non-emphasized numbers are "go-alongs," or Minors for that Code. You will refer to these Codes when you pick lucky digits for names.

Code No. 1	179*	134	438	555	Code No. 21	867*	497	632	359
Code No. 2	448*	229	336	543	Code No. 22	537*	648	342	428
Code No. 3	771*	639	223	229	Code No. 23	438*	328	754	496
Code No. 4	333*	120	109	201	Code No. 24	339*	253	424	649
Code No. 5	189*	274	324	654	Code No. 25	542*	749	648	337
Code No. 6	790*	552	269	139	Code No. 26	116*	438	635	771
Code No. 7	888*	104	210	665	Code No. 27	889*	674	299	546
Code No. 8	149*	136	709	435	Code No. 28	616*	428	645	743
Code No. 9	118*	333	634	106	Code No. 29	665*	563	794	330
Code No. 10	142*	224	578	941	Code No. 30	842*	327	496	397
Code No. 11	439*	240	592	521	Code No. 31	559*	437	604	109
Code No. 12	118*	107	886	439	Code No. 32	770*	183	407	557
Code No. 13	648*	517	739	531	Code No. 33	332*	864	409	647
Code No. 14	390*	247	519	620	Code No. 34	380*	406	883	462
Code No. 15	180*	221	485	339	Code No. 35	275*	056	372	548
Code No. 16	888*	675	109	756	Code No. 36	934*	607	249	954
Code No. 17	177*	435	498	624	Code No. 37	439*	666	603	492
Code No. 18	337*	238	530	639	Code No. 38	253*	652	808	509
Code No. 19	543*	762	852	444	Code No. 39	677*	482	587	374
Code No. 20	334*	229	724	123	Code No. 40	404*	125	672	777

FINDING A WINNING NUMBER BY MEANS OF A NAME

To analyze a name for winning numbers, we first print the name, and underneath each letter we place the number that the letter vibrates to:

$$\begin{array}{ccccccccc} J & O & H & N & S & M & I & T & H \\ 1 & 6 & 8 & 5 & 1 & 4 & 9 & 2 & 8 \end{array}$$

Add all the figures in the first name: 1 plus 6 plus 8 plus 5 = **20.**
Take all the figures in the second name: 1 plus 4 plus 2 plus 8 = **24.**
Reduce the 20, which represents JOHN, in this way: 2 plus 0 = **2.**
Reduce the 24, which represents SMITH, like this: 2 plus 4 = **6.**
Add the 2 of JOHN to the 6 of SMITH to get a total: 2 plus 6 = **8.**

So **8** is JOHN SMITH's Destiny Number. This is useful for a character analysis, but betting systems require more than a single digit. Here are two popular ways to derive additional digits:

EXAMINE THE WORK-OUT FOR COMBINATIONS

In producing the above work-out on the name JOHN SMITH, note the numbers in bold type, namely **20-24-2-6-8.** There is more than one way to parse these, but given that **8** is his Destiny Number, let's use **0-2-4-6** as Minors, and he will have many fruitful two- and three-digit combinations to play, among them 20, 24, 26, 68, 202, 242, 268, 426, 624, 862, and 888.

EMPLOY THE MASTER CODE AS A RUN-DOWN SYSTEM

We can apply a run-down or derivative system on JOHN SMITH's Destiny Number, which is **8.** As has been made clear, there are a great many popular run-down systems, but here we will apply the simple Lewis de Claremont Master Code run-down from the previous page.

Code No. 8   149*   136   709   435

This run-down gives JOHN SMITH four three-digit betting numbers, (149, 136, 709, 435) with **149** emphasized as especially lucky.

HOW TO INTERPRET DREAMS AND THOUGHTS
SO AS TO GIVE YOU WINNING NUMBERS

The Master Code is not intended to replace your favourite dream book, but in one page it provides a wide variety of mystically-generated numbers you can apply to virtually every vision, thought, or situation.

To use it is simplicity itself. Start by determining the principal part of your dream, vision, or thought — any word or any group of words that impressed you the most. If you prefer, choose instead any unusual scene that struck you strongly as you went about your daily tasks.

Once you have your word or phrase in mind, write it out and place underneath each letter the number as indicated by the Master Code and work it out for yourself. Say that perhaps you dreamed of a Snake and wish to turn this dream into a lucky number.

S N A K E
1 5 1 2 5

1 plus 5 plus 1 plus 2 plus 5 = **14**

But 14 is not the only number you can derive from this word. Because we have Master Codes from 1 through 40, it follows that in deciding the proper vibration that this 14 fits into, we do not need to reduce it to one digit. In other words, we do not need to add 1 and 4 to get 5, but we can accept 14 as the final number and look into the Master Code to see what winning numbers No. 14 generates. And then we can also add 1 plus 4 = 5 and generate a second set of three-digit numbers:

Code No. 14	390*	247	519	620
Code No. 5	189*	274	324	654

Note that aside from the strong vibrations associated with the asterisked numbers 390* and 189*, the seemingly arbitrary choice to examine the codes for both 14 and 5 has placed two similar numbers in close proximity, one beneath the other: **247** and **274**.

This highly suggestive combination also brings up permutations, such as **472, 427, 724**, and **742,** which well may be fortunate for betting.

MORE DREAMS AND VISIONS

Let us try working out a few more dreams, signs, and omens.

$$M \quad U \quad D \quad D \quad Y \quad \quad W \quad A \quad T \quad E \quad R$$
$$4 \quad 3 \quad 4 \quad 4 \quad 7 \quad \quad 5 \quad 1 \quad 2 \quad 5 \quad 9$$

4 plus 3 plus 4 plus 4 plus 7 = 22. **MUDDY** has **5** letters and = **22**.
5 plus 1 plus 2 plus 5 plus 9 = 22. **WATER** has **5** letters and = **22**.

Now this is an important fact: When a phrase consists of two words with the identical number of letters, and the summed numbers for the two words are exactly the same, and especially when both are Master Numbers, it is a very strong omen that must not be overlooked or altered. You could bet this dream as **522**, or you could look under No. 22 in the Number Code:

Code No. 22   537*   648   342   428

$$D \quad E \quad A \quad D \quad \quad P \quad E \quad R \quad S \quad O \quad N$$
$$4 \quad 5 \quad 1 \quad 4 \quad \quad 7 \quad 5 \quad 9 \quad 1 \quad 6 \quad 5$$

4 plus 5 plus 1 plus 4 = 14, then 1 plus 4 = 5. DEAD = **5**
7 plus 5 plus 9 plus 1 plus 6 plus 5 = 33. PERSON = **33**
5 plus 33 = 38, so look under No. 38 in the Number Code:

Code No. 38   253*   652   808   509

$$L \quad O \quad S \quad I \quad N \quad G \quad \quad M \quad O \quad N \quad E \quad Y$$
$$3 \quad 6 \quad 1 \quad 9 \quad 5 \quad 7 \quad \quad 4 \quad 6 \quad 5 \quad 5 \quad 7$$

3 plus 6 plus 1 plus 9 plus 5 plus 7 = 31. LOSING = **31.**
4 plus 6 plus 5 plus 5 plus 7 = 27. MONEY = **27.**
31 plus 27 = 58; 5 plus 8 = 13, so look at No. 13 in the Number Code:

Code No. 13   648*   517   739   531

The de Claremont Code has been enjoyed for years, but you can create your own code. Name your dream, number it, and check what number won. Keep a record and build your own code, dream by dream, and win by win.

CHAPTER TWENTY
YOUR LUCKY LO SHU LOTTERY NUMBERS

HOW TO BET ON YOUR THREE-DIGIT LO SHU LINES

Asian gamblers like to catch lucky numbers from *The Interpretation of Dreams by the Duke of Zhou*, which divides dreams into more than a dozen catagories — such as Straight, Contrary, Happy, Personal, Seasonal, Illness, and Ghost Dreams — and then provides a pair of four-digit numbers for each dream-vision. But dream-numbers are not the only way to find digits to bet by using Chinese-style Numerology.

Experienced numbers-players who have learned through this book how to work out their Birth Date Numbers in the Magic Square in order to derive a character analysis may already be anticipating this next adaptation of the Lo Shu or Saturn Square, and it will not disappoint. YES! The three-digit lucky lines in your Lo Shu Square can be used in any lottery system that requires three-digit numbers. Here's how:

- **Positive Line Numbers:** Any three-digit positive line in your own personal Magic Square is a combo you can play. Just as in a Westtern Numerology draw-down, these numbers are your MAJORS. You may have more than one positive line, giving you multiple three-digit combinations; if so, you are a very lucky person. Also try this: Work up a Magic Square for the date-of-play and see what positive lines it brings forth. You can play the lines in either direction, as you choose.

- **"Loose" Numbers:** Numbers that appear "loose" in your own personal Chinese Magic Square, but do not form part of a positive line, are similar to your MINORS in Western Numerology draw-downs. Use them when you feel them, but don't rely on them.

- **Negative Arrow Numbers:** Compare any three-digit negative arrow in your birth date Square (or the Square for date-of-play) against the basic Magic Square. The row of "missing numbers" may be noted as an UN-lucky numerical combination that you may avoid placing bets on, unless you are one of those bold souls who takes personal delight in betting on "reverse bad luck" numbers such as 13 and 666.

CHAPTER TWENTY-ONE
WHEN TO BET:
YOUR LUCKY YEARS AND LUCKY DAYS

BETTING BIGGER DURING YOUR LUCKY YEARS

Lucky years are those in which happy coincidences occur with unusual frequency, unhappy coincidences are minimal, and there is a tendency to win unusually often, or unusually high sums of money, when gambling.

LUCKY YEARS BY BIRTH DATE AND ELAPSED AGE

Earlier we worked out yearly situational predictions for RANDOLPH JOHN WILLIAMS, and noted that his lucky Birth Date Number is **3**.

Now, to find his lucky Personal Years, which run from birthday to birthday, we will search his name for 3s. Beneath the numbers of the name are his age-numbers, according to the system of year-by-year forecasts.

```
R   A   N   D   O   L   P   H    J   O   H   N    W   I   L   L   I   A   M   S
9   1   5   4   6   3   7   8    1   6   8   5    5   9   3   3   9   1   4   1
Age 1  2   3   4   5   6   7   8    9  10  11  12   13  14  15  16  17  18  19  20
Age 21 22  23  24  25  26  27  28   29  30  31  32   33  34  35  36  37  38  39  40
```

His 6th, 15th, 16th, 26th, 35th, and 36th years, all vibrating to number **3**, are lucky years for him. In these years he may win at games of chance.

LUCKY YEARS BY BIRTH DATE AND CURRENT YEAR

A second method to find lucky years, generally considered to indicate minor wins, is to compare the Birth Date Number against upcoming years, after reducing them to one digit. As noted previously, JANE ELIZABETH BROWN's birth date reduces to **4**, but she has no 4s, and hence no lucky years, in her name. However, 4 does appear in a regular sequence in her life, as the years 1921, 1930, 1939, and 1948 all reduce to **4**. The reason this system is relegated to minor wins is that the current year number appears to everyone. It is before the general public, and not personal to her.

LUCKY YEARS BY ELAPSED AGE PLUS CURRENT YEAR

The luckiest betting years are found by combining the two systems above. We will take up again the case of RANDOLPH JOHN WILLIAMS, born April 8th, 1917, with a Birth Date Number of **3**. We will add two more rows of age-dates, to find his exceptionally lucky years, when his elapsed age coincides with a **3** in his name, and his Personal Year, running from his birthday to the end of the calendar year, also reduces to his lucky **3**.

R	A	N	D	O	L	P	H		J	O	H	N		W	I	L	L	I	A	M	S
9	1	5	4	6	**3**	7	8		1	6	8	5		5	9	**3**	**3**	9	1	4	1

*Age 1 2 3 4 5 **6** 7 8   9 10 11 12   13 14 **15 16** 17 18 19 20*
*Age 21 22 23 24 25 **26** 27 28   29 30 31 32   33 34 **35 36** 37 38 39 40*
*Age 41 42 43 44 45 **46** 47 48   49 50 51 52   53 54 **55 56** 57 58 59 60*
*Age 61 62 63 64 65 **66** 67 68   69 70 71 72   73 74 **75 76** 77 78 79 80*

On his first lucky year, when he was 6, but the current year was 1923, which reduces to 6. His second lucky year, when he was 15, was 1932, which reduces to 6 as well. The rest of the years are here in chart form:

1917	1917	1917	1917	1917	1917	1917	1917	1917
+ 16	+ 26	+ 35	+ 36	+ 46	+ 55	+ 56	+ 66	+ 75
1933	1943	1952	1953	1963	1972	1973	1983	1992
7	8	8	9	1	1	2	**3**	**3**

His 66th and 75th years are when he can play long shots — and win!

BETTING CONSISTENTLY ON YOUR LUCKY DAYS

Not all years will be lucky ones for you, but if you like to play, you will want to make the best of the less-fortunate years, and to make the most of your lucky years. This is where the plan of placing small bets on lucky days comes in — and just as with the several systems of determining lucky years, there are varied systems for picking lucky days.

Many people simply look up the lucky day of the week for their Astrology sign; we offer both the de Claremont Master Code system, and several alternative methods of interest from *The Mystic Fortune Teller.*

FIND YOUR LUCKY DAY TO BET BY NAME OR DREAM

If your name is a 1, check Master Code No. 1 on page 81, where 179 is emphasized. Add 1 plus 7 plus 9 = 17. Reduce 17 to **8**. Number 8 is **Sunday**, so Sunnday is your Lucky Name Day to bet.

To derive Lucky Dream Days, sum the Dream Keyword, check the Master Code, reduce it, and that is the day to play, until you dream again.

Included here are also some old prognostications from *The Mystic Fortune Teller* regarding children born on certain days.

SUNDAY: Number 1 and Number 8, Sun, Sign: Leo
A child born on Sunday shall be of long life and obtain riches either by industry or by inheritance, or, perchance, by both means.

MONDAY: Number 2 and Number 9, Moon, Sign: Cancer
A child born on Monday will be physically weak but will also be spiritually sensitive in like measure to any bodily shortcoming.

TUESDAY: Number 3, Mars, Signs: Aries and Scorpio
Tuesday is unfortunate for children, though a child born on this day may, by extraordinary vigilance, conquer the danger of a violent death.

WEDNESDAY: Number 4, Mercury, Signs: Gemini and Virgo
The child born on Wednesday will be given to a studious, intellectual life, with far-reaching thoughts, and shall reap great profit therefrom.

THURSDAY: Number 5, Jupiter, Signs: Sagittarius and Pisces
The child born on Thursday shall attain great honour and dignity, but must be wary of gaining weight excessively through indulgence.

FRIDAY: Number 6, Venus, Signs: Taurus and Libra
The child who has Friday as the natal day shall be of a lovely, strong constitution, and perhaps addicted to the pleasures of love.

SATURDAY: Number 7, Saturn, Signs: Capricorn and Aquarius
Saturday is an ill-omened day; most children born on this day will be of heavy, dull, and dogged disposition, albeit they will be hard workers.

HOW TO DETERMINE THE LUCKY AND THE UNLUCKY DAYS OF ANY MONTH IN THE YEAR

This method of finding out each month's lucky days by the date of the Full Moon comes to us from *The Mystic Fortune Teller,* one of many mini-booklets published by Wehman Bros. of New York. The publication date is 1911, but this text is probably British, not American, and it certainly dates back to the 19th century.

Using this system requires a small amount of mathematical creativity, as well as an awareness of the date of the month's Full Moon, but its great usefulness is that it frees the user from having to consult the lucky days found in dream books, which are static from year to year. Static dates tend to be over-bet by the general public, because so many people consider them lucky, and over-betting lowers one's chances of success on those days.

THE LUCKY DAYS BY MONTH AND MOON

Ascertain from the Almanac the day on which a Full Moon occurs, and count the number of days from that to the end of the calendar month. You then multiply the number of days in the month by the number ascertained as above, and the product will give you the month's lucky days, subject to a further test hereafter explained.

Let us take as an example a Full Moon that occurs on the 13th of the month of June, a month which is 30 days long, leaving 17 days to the end of the month as the multiplier. The product of 17 times 30 is 510, so the lucky days of that particular June would be the 5th and the 10th, if no tests worked to the contrary.

If your product should be an unlikely calendrical choice, like 501, the days would be the same, the 5th and the 10th, for you may transpose figures that are out of order, so that they work together to make two logical dates, which are, as always, subject to your tests.

Suppose, that, instead of 510, the product should be 899. This would occur in a 31-day month if the Full Moon fell on the 2nd, leaving 29 for the multiplier, as 29 times 31 is 899. Neither of these figures can be paired to make a single-digit and a double-digit date, so the lucky days for that month are the 8th and the 9th, and the 9th would be considered doubly lucky, if no tests worked to the contrary.

TESTING LUCKY DAYS BY MEANS OF UNLUCKY DAYS

After working out your list of lucky days, you must then test them, in order to be sure that there are no opposing influences. You can do this by calculating the unlucky days — which are determined in precisely the same manner, except that you will multiply the number of days in the month by the number which had passed *previous* to the Full Moon. In our example, the Full Moon fell on the 13th, so there were 12 days previous, to be multiplied by 30, the number of days in the month. The sum is 360. The unlucky days are the 3rd and the 6th.

Should you ever find that any day of the month which was designated as lucky came also in the list of unlucky days, the latter preponderates, and you must strike it from the lucky list. In this case, 3 and 6 do not cancel out 5 or 10, so our lucky days have proven true.

This plan of demonstrating lucky and unlucky days is very ancient, and has been tested to such an extent that it is considered accurate. In olden times, before the mass of people understood much about figures, fortune tellers demanded a large fee for casting the lucky days of any month.

LUCKY DAYS FOR A MARRIAGE

Lucky marriage days for girls are cast in this same manner, except that the age of the girl is used as the multiplier, instead of the number of days in the month. The result is confirmed by a test of the unlucky days.

Thus, if a girl is 18 years old, and thinks of marrying in October, she takes up an Almanac and ascertains the day of a Full Moon in that month. It occurs on the 24th, and there are 31 days in the month. This leaves 7 for the multiplier. She multiplies this 7 by her age, 18, and the result is 126, which shows the lucky days in that month for her to marry are the 1st and 26th, as well as the 12th and 6th, unless they are destroyed by the test, which is determined as follows:

There are 23 days before the 24th, and she must multiply 23 by her age of 18, which gives 414, which shows that the 4th and 14th are the only unlucky days for her to marry in that particular month; and as they do not conflict with the lucky days, the 1st, 6th, 12th, and 26th may be considered as her genuine lucky marriage days for that month, reckoning the Moon to have fulled on the 24th.

CHAPTER TWENTY-TWO
GEMATRIA AND OTHER "CABALISMS"

ANCIENT SCRIPTURAL NUMEROLOGY

The *Sefer Yetzirah (Book of Formation)*, is the earliest extant text of Jewish esotericism. The title is a pun on *sefer* (a book), *sefor* (a count), *sippur* (a story), and *sephirot* (attributes). Written in the 2nd century, its subject is Gematria, a type of Numerology that links the 22 letters of the Hebrew alphabet, God's 10 *sephirot* (attributes), and 32 ways or paths whereby God made the Universe. Understanding it is said to enable a pious practitioner to create life — such as the *golem*, a mud-monster animated by Judah Lœw ben Bezalel, the Maharal of Prague, in the 16th century.

Although the practice of Gematria originated in Assyro-Babylonian culture, and the word itself was originally Greek, in the Hebrew language Gematria describes an alphanumeric code in which a number is assigned to each Hebrew letter, and words are then enumerated, reduced, and evaluated. One of the basic principles of Gematria is that all words that share the same numerical value have a hidden or esoteric relationship to one another, and that through this code, the transformation of seemingly unrelated words into sets of numerically identical words expresses subtle relational information about the formation of the Universe.

Gematria was first used to identify the same-numbered words in the Bible, but it has also been applied to scriptural phrases, angelic names, the names and attributes of God, and a variety of religious and secular texts.

The study of Gematria eventually came to be included in the Kabbalah, a form of Jewish occultism that originated in the Middle Ages and is still popular to this day. Kabbalistic Gematria employs various techniques to derive the unique number values of words, including numerical reduction, squaring each number, and multiplying the value of each number by its position in the word before addition and reduction.

In Greek culture, the term for this form of same-identity Numerology is Isopsephy, which translates as "an equal number of pebbles" (meaning that the numbers are the same). It is applied to the 27-letter Greek alphabet.

In Arabic Numerology, the Abjad numerals, corresponding to the 28 letters of the Arabic alphabet, are used for a similar technique of transformative and spiritually relational Numerology.

THE HEBREW ALPHABET IN NUMBERS

The Hebrew alphabet consists of 22 letters, plus five letters that have special numerical values when they appear as the final letter in a word. The system is quite elegant, but it is only useful if you fluently speak and write Hebrew, which is not the case for most people, and not even for all Jews.

1 Aleph א	10 Yod י	100 Koof ק
2 Bet ב	20 Kaf כ	200 Reish ר
3 Gimel ג	30 Lamed ל	300 Shin ש
4 Daleth ד	40 Mem מ	400 Taf ת
5 Heh ה	50 Nun נ	500 Kaf (final) ך
6 Vav ו	60 Samech ס	600 Mem (final) ם
7 Zayin ז	70 Ayin ע	700 Nun (final) ן
8 Het ח	80 Peh פ	800 Peh (final) ף
9 Tet ט	90 Tzadi צ	900 Tzadi (final) ץ

DOWN-HOME BIBLICAL "NUMBEROLOGY"

Christian mystics, especially native English-speakers, have long been fascinated by the Jewish Kabbalah, but of course they want to decipher the "Bible Code" into English — and for doctrinal reasons, many restrict their study to the King James Bible in particular. Given their strong interest, a form of substitute Hebrew Gematria has arisen in Great Britain and North America that employs conventional Numerology, adapted for use with the Christian Bible and the English alphabet of 26 letters.

Oddly, although the word Gematria entered the English language in the 17th century, during the late 19th and early 20th centuries, when it was commonplace for Anglophones to spell the word Kabbalah as Cabala, English-language Biblical Gematria was often called "Cabalism" by Numerologists, and some American authors, perhaps less literate than they ought to have been, called their Biblical decodings "Numberology."

As a Jew, i sometimes wonder why so many Christians have tried their hand at English Biblical Gematria, but i cannot fault them, for just like Rabbi Akiva, who may (or may not) have written the *Sefer Yetzirah*, they are searching for a way to identify the numerical relatedness of words from the Bible, a task of great spiritual meaning to the faithful.

WORDS LINKED BY SHARED NUMBER VALUES

Among the most original thinkers in American Cabalism was a man named Frank Householder. His *Four Basic Principles of Numerology: Efficiency of the Five Kingdoms,* published in 1921, is almost impenetrably dense and crankish, but for all of its obvious eccentricities, it is a pure expression of English Gematria for the masses.

Householder concerned himself with words found in the King James Bible and with scientific terminology. In his work-outs, the final digit (that is, 1 through 9) is of primary importance, but the second-to-final number is considered too. For example, the number 6 may be derived in several ways, including from 24 (2 plus 4 = 6) or 33 (3 plus 3 = 6), but the words that "got there the same way" are considered to be more closely related than those that took another path to the destination.

A few samples of Householder's work explain why he believed — and how he sought to prove — that certain words are *spiritually* related.

T R U T H	J U S T I C E
2 9 3 2 8	1 3 1 2 9 3 5
24	**24**
6	**6**

O M N I P O T E N T	E V E R L A S T I N G
6 4 5 9 7 6 2 5 5 2	5 4 5 9 3 1 1 2 9 5 7
51	**51**
6	**6**

I M M O R T A L M I N D	C O N S C I O U S L I F E
9 4 4 6 9 2 1 3 4 9 6 4	3 6 5 1 3 9 6 3 1 3 9 6 5
60	**60**
6	**6**

On the next page you will find alphabetical lists of words for each number. Householder produced many, many pages of these lists, but the present selection, consisting of one "alphabet" for each final number, should suffice to show his method. I hope and trust it will open the eyes of those who may wish to make a study of English-language Gematria.

WORDS THAT ARE SPIRITUALLY RELATED
BY VIRTUE OF IDENTICAL NUMERICAL VALUES

- **1:** Adept, Balm, Calvary, Dare, Egg, Forgive, Guide, Heaven, Integrity, Jewel, Kingdom, Liberty, Mercy, Number, Omniscience, Paradise, Quest, Reliable, Sky, Teach, Union, Vitality, Worthy, Young, Zion.

- **2:** Accursed, Bedlam, Cross, Death, Eden, Famine, Gold, Harlot, Immense, Jesus, Kindred, Leper, Malady, Near, Ointment, Psychic, Quarrel, Respect, Speech, Tempt, Unbelief, Vulture, Wisdom, Yellow.

- **3:** Abide, Beget, Charity, Daughter, Envy, Family, Gaze, Harvest, Idle, Join, Kine, Loosen, Marry, Nazarene, Ox, Peace, Question, Reproach, Son, Thief, Uncouth, Veil, Wedding, Yoke.

- **4:** Absolve, Blot, Captive, Design, Enlighten, Father, Garden, Honey, Idol, Judgement, Kiss, Lord, Master, Night, Omnipresent, Potential, Quit, Relieve, Sustain, Thirst, Universal, Vault, Water, Year, Zodiac.

- **5:** Anchor, Brother, Christ, Dead, Emblem, Flesh, Gall, Hill, Icon, Joy, Key, Leaven, Memorial, Nourish, Obligation, Prophesy, Quench, Redeem, Sacred, Touchstone, Universe, Vine, Wound, Xray, Years.

- **6:** Amen, Believe, Consider, Diamond, Everlasting, Feast, Genesis, Holy, Incense, Justice, Knowledge, Lamp, Magic, New, Omnipotent, Pledge, Quality, Repent, Sin, Trial, Uphold, Vow, Word, Zone.

- **7:** All, Bliss, Church, Devil, Empty, False, Grace, Humanity, Impiety, Just, Kennel, Lenient, Mother, Nature, Ordain, Psalm, Quick, Remember, Sinner, Throne, Virgin, Wrath, Your, Zinc.

- **8:** Abhor, Ban, Cosmic, Doubt, Exalt, Faith, God, Hope, Immaculate, Jubilant, Kinetic, Letter, Mystery, Narrow, Obedience, Prophet, Queen, Raiment, Spiritual, Temple, Unity, Vast, Whisper, Zephyr.

- **9:** Able, Breath, Child, Deity, Evolve, Fortune, Grateful, Health, Inspiration, Journey, Knock, Love, Money, Nail, Oil, Path, Quiet, Reason, Sun, Thought, Upright, Vindicate, Worship, Yearn, Zealous.

SUCCESS • HAPPINESS
LOVE • MONEY • LIFE

The study of the SCIENCE OF NUMBERS (Numerology) helps develop certain faculties in you that should lead greatly towards bringing success into your life — success in the solving of your problems, your love affairs, your financial plight.

To understand — to interpret and excel in the Science Of Numbers — you must exercise your ANALYTICAL powers, you must OBSERVE things, and you must use your INTUITIVE faculties.

You must study people — study things — you must observe things about you — not merely "see" but observe with an inner eye — then analyze and use the intuitive faculty that it is believed the Lord gave all of us. All this leads to a better understanding, not only of Numerology, but all your life problems.

If this booklet has done only just that — exercised your powers of OBSERVATION, ANALYSIS, and INTUITION; if this booklet has made you realize the importance of using these powers — then you and I have been greatly repaid.

— LEWIS de CLAREMONT

Read more about Mr. Young here: **LuckyMojo.com/young.html**

GOOD LUCK AND HAPPY NUMBERING!

Numerology and Arithmancy have been among my passions since i was a child, and i hope that this book will convey my enthusiasm and my knowledge to succeeding generations of "Numberologists."

I have placed a great deal of my own original research in this book, but in closing i wish again to acknowledge the foundational teachings of Dr. Roy Page Walton, the Anonymous Wehman Bros. Author, the Mysterious Mr. Young (Lewis de Claremont, Godfrey Spencer), Robert A. Nelson (Dr. Korda RaMayne), Mrs. L. Dow Balliett, Walter B. Gibson, Lillian Too, Frank Householder, and the other authors named in the Bibliography.

Whether you use this information for the purposes of character analysis or for betting, i wish you all the luck in the world!

— catherine yronwode

BIBLIOGRAPHY

Adams, Karen. *Numerology Up-To-Date: A Key to Your Fate.* Herbert Jenkins Ltd., 1926.

Balliett, L. Dow, Mrs. *How to Attain Success Through the Strength of Vibration: A System of Numbers as Taught by Pythagoras.* Balliett, 1905.

Balliett, L. Dow, Mrs. *The Philosophy of Numbers: Their Tone and Colors.* Balliett, 1908.

Berglund, Lars. *The Secret of Luo Shu: Numerology in Chinese Art and Architecture.* Institutionen för Konstvetenskap, 1990.

Campbell, Helen; Knox, Thomas; Byrnes, Thomas. *Darkness and Daylight; or, Lights and Shadows of New York Life.* A. D. Worthington & Co., 1892.

Cheasley, Clifford W. *Numerology: Its Practical Application to Life.* Clifford W. Cheasley, 1914.

Cheasley, Clifford W. *Numbers: What's In Your Name?* Edward J. Clode, 1916.

Cheasley, Clifford W. *Numerology at a Glance.* Clifford W. Cheasley, 1932..

Cheiro [Count Louis Hamon]. *The Book of Numbers.* Herbert Jenkins, 1926. Revised as *Cheiro's Book of Numbers.* Herbert Jenkins, 1927, Barrie & Jenkins, 1978.

De Claremont, Lewis [pseud.]. *How To Get Your Winning Number.* Empire Publishing, 1938.

Gibson, Walter B. *The Science of Numerology: What Numbers Mean To You.* George Sully & Co., 1927.

Householder, Frank. *Four Basic Principles of Numerology:Efficiency of the Five Kingdoms.* Seaside Publishing Co. 1921.

Jordan, Juno. *Numerology: The Romance in Your Name.* J.F. Rowny Press, 1965; Reprinted, DeVorss & Co., 1973.

Kozminsky, Isidore. *Numbers, Their Meaning and Magic.* G. P. Putnam's Sons, 1927.

Lip, Evelyn. *Chinese Numbers: Significance, Symbolism, and Traditions.* Times Editions, 1992.

Madison, Malcolm. *Numerology.* Tower Books Inc., 1930.

Ottley, Roi. *Inside Black America.* Eyre and Spottiswoode, 1948.

Perez, Dennis. *You Can Learn the Lo Shu Square!* Perez, 2010.

RaMayne, Korda [Robert A. Nelson]. *Korda RaMayne's Mystic Key to Numerology: Science of Numbers.* Nelson Enterprises, 1931.

Sepharial [Walter Gorn Old]. *The Kabala of Numbers.* (2 Vols.) Rider, 1911, 1913. MacKay, 1928.

Shafton, Anthony. *Dream Singers: The African American Way with Dreams.* J. Wiley, 2002.

Spencer, Godfrey [pseud.]. *The Secret of Numbers Revealed: The Magic Power of Numbers.* Empire / Pyramid / Dorene Publishing, 1938,1939; Dorene revised edition, 1969.

Taylor, Ariel Yvon. *Numerology Made Plain: The Science of Names and Numbers and the Law of Vibration.* Laidlaw Brothers, 1930.

Thompson, Nathan. *Kings: The True Story of Chicago's Policy Kings and Numbers Racketeers: An Informal History.* The Bronzeville Press, 2006.

Too, Lillian. *Chinese Numerology in Feng Shui.* Konsep Lagenda Books, 1994.

Walton, Dr. Roy Page. *Names, Dates, and Numbers: What They Mean To You.* Edward J. Clode, 1914.

White, Shane; Garton, Stephen; Robertson, Stephen; White, Graham. *Playing the Numbers: Gambling in Harlem Between the Wars.* Harvard University Press, 2010.

Webster, Richard. *Chinese Numerology: The Way to Prosperity & Fulfillment.* Llewellyn, 1998.

Wehman Bros. [pseud.] *Mystic Fortune Teller.* Wehman Bros. 1911.

Westcott, William Wynn. *Numbers: Their Occult Power and Mystic Virtue.* Theosophical Publishing House, 1890, 1911, etc.; Reprint, 1974.

See also the YIPPIE Numerology Bibliography: **Yronwode.org/numerology-bibliography.html**